2·50

PARAMAHANSA YOGANANDA

A photograph taken an hour before his *mahasamadhi* (a yogi's final conscious exit from the body) at a banquet held in honor of Ambassador Sen of India, March 7, 1952, the Biltmore Hotel, Los Angeles.

The photographer has here caught a loving smile that appears to be a farewell benediction for each one of the master's millions of friends, students, and disciples. The eyes that already were gazing into Eternity are yet full of human warmth and understanding.

PARAMAHANSA YOGANANDA

In Memoriam

The Master's Life, Work, and Mahasamadhi

SELF-REALIZATION FELLOWSHIP
Founded by Paramahansa Yogananda

Authorized by the International Publications
Council of Self-Realization Fellowship

Self-Realization Fellowship was founded in 1920 by Paramahansa Yogananda to be the instrument for the worldwide dissemination of his
teachings. The reader can be certain of the authenticity of writings and
recordings by or about Paramahansa Yogananda and his teachings if the
registered Self-Realization emblem, and/or the statement of authoriza-
tion (shown together above), appears on that work.

Printed in the United States of America
ISBN-0-87612-170-9

10211-65432

CONTENTS

The *Mahasamadhi* of a World Teacher 9

Tribute from Dr. W. Y. Evans-Wentz 23

Tribute from Mme. Amelita Galli-Curci 35

Tribute from Swami Sivananda of Rishikesh 51

When I Am Only a Dream (*poem*) 62
    BY PARAMAHANSA YOGANANDA

Tributes from Ambassador of India 64

Last Speech of Paramahansa Yogananda 67

Tribute from *New Age Interpreter* 69

Banquet Guests, Hotel Biltmore, March 7, 1952 (*picture*) 72

Thoughts at Last Public Rites 75

Life and Work of Paramahansa Yogananda 77

Memorial Services in India 85

To Guruji (*poem*) 91
    BY GRACE THOMPSON SETON

Why Does a Great Master Suffer? 93

An Appreciation by M. R. Ahuja, Consul General of India . . . 98

Paramahansa Yogananda: *In Memoriam* 100
    BY SAROJ KUMAR DAS, PH.D.

Yoga and the Miracle of Incorruption 105

Tribute from Goodwin J. Knight, Governor of California . . . 115

Tributes from Friends and Self-Realization Centers 116

Letter from Forest Lawn Memorial-Park 121

PARAMAHANSA YOGANANDA

The last photograph of Paramahansa Yogananda, taken a few minutes before his death, shows the wife of the Ambassador of India respectfully pronaming to him. India thus symbolically expressed through her a heartfelt gratitude to its great son in the West.

The Mahasamadhi of a World Teacher

On March 7, 1952, Paramahansa Yogananda
Left the Body for Omnipresence

On March 7, 1952, the incarnation of Paramahansa Yogananda came to a perfect close. A life without blemish ended in *mahasamadhi* (a yogi's final conscious exit from the body). Death took place at 9:30 p.m., a few moments after Paramahansaji had uttered the final words in a speech at the Biltmore Hotel in Los Angeles. Unstintingly he gave of himself to the very end, to the last breath of his life.

Born a *Kshatriya* (a member of the second Hindu caste, originally that of kings and warriors), Yoganandaji died as he had lived: a divine warrior against the chief foe of man — ignorance.

Paramahansaji's last days were literally and symbolically bound up with the visit to Los Angeles of the Ambassador of India at that time, Mr. Binay Ranjan Sen. The great guru could not go to India, so India — in the person of her highest foreign representative — came to the guru.

The last photograph of Yoganandaji, taken a few minutes before his death, shows the Ambassador's wife *pronaming** to him as he rose from his seat to go to the speaker's stand. By that last beautiful gesture, an Indian woman symbolized the respect of her nation for the man who, more than any other son of India, made the perennial wisdom of the *rishis*† known and loved in the West.

---

* A *pronam* (literally, "complete bowing down") is a gesture of greeting among Hindus; it consists in joining one's hands, palms touching each other. The *pronam* in India takes the place of the Western greeting by handshaking.

† The *rishis* (lit., "seers") were India's ancient sages to whom the *Vedas* were revealed.

A letter from the Mortuary Director of Forest Lawn Memorial-Park, one of America's largest and most beautiful cemeteries, appears on pp. 121-124 incl. of this booklet. He testifies that Yoganandaji's body remained "in a phenomenal state of immutability." For weeks after the Master's passing, his unchanged face shone with the divine luster of incorruptibility. This miracle appears to have taken place through the grace of the Heavenly Father, that men might know the goodness of Yoganandaji's mission on earth. The beautiful phenomena attending Paramahansaji's death have aroused world interest in the soul-revealing possibilities of yoga.

Yoganandaji came to America to fulfill a specific mission, that of spreading in the West a knowledge of yoga techniques by which man can enter into conscious communion with his Creator. Paramahansaji was the last in a line of four gurus * who were divinely inspired — directly commanded by God — to teach openly to the modern world the secret yogic science of self-liberation that was the glory of ancient India.

"Kriya Yoga, the scientific technique of God-realization, will ultimately spread in all lands, and aid in harmonizing the nations through man's personal, transcendental perception of the Infinite Father." With these words Mahavatar Babaji sent Yoganandaji, in 1920, to the West.

The young monk — trained for his high duty for ten years at the Indian hermitage of his guru, Sri Yukteswarji — labored lovingly for more than thirty years in the New World, honoring the trust of the great humanitarian masters behind him. To them and to God, Master† gave all credit for the successful execution of his mission.

"After my passing," Paramahansaji said, "the SRF teachings will be the guru." By these words and in many other ways he indicated that the

---

* The line of four gurus: Mahavatar Babaji, who is still living in the Himalayas; Lahiri Mahasaya (1828-1895), who gave initiation to 5000 *Kriya Yoga* disciples in India; Sri Yukteswar (1855-1936), who trained Yoganandaji for his mission in the West; and Paramahansa Yogananda.

† Yoganandaji is called "Master" by his disciples. In India the suffix "ji" ("conqueror" of oneself) is added to names of venerated persons; hence, Paramahansaji, Yoganandaji, Swamiji, Guruji, etc. The *Guru Gita,* sloka 17, aptly refers to the meaning of guru as *gu,* "darkness," *ru,* "that which dispels"; i.e., "dispeller of darkness."

practical interest in yoga which he had initiated in the West would continue to grow after his death. Like all other men of God, Master did not emphasize the importance of his own personality but rather the necessity of one's own struggle to achieve the life beautiful.

"'Divine union,' the *Yogavatar* [Lahiri Mahasaya] proclaimed, 'is possible through self-effort, and is not dependent on theological beliefs or on the arbitrary will of a Cosmic Dictator.' Through use of the *Kriya* key, persons who cannot bring themselves to believe in the divinity of any man will behold at last the full divinity of their own selves."*

During his last three years Paramahansaji withdrew more and more from public life in order to devote himself fully to literary work: editing and revision of his earlier books and the completion of new writings. Shortly before his death he said to a disciple: "My life work is done."

Great devotees of God, the Hindu scriptures tell us, are given fore-warning of the time of their departure from this earth. A true yogi, unlike the unenlightened man, is never rudely surprised by Death. Yoganandaji had been aware of the general plan of his life ever since his youthful years with his omniscient guru, Sri Yukteswar. Master well knew his life would not be a long one. "I shall not live to be old," he told a disciple in 1924.

Paramahansaji gave a number of close disciples many hints that he would pass on in March 1952. They did not understand the full implication of his words. It seemed impossible that, for them, a morning was fast approaching when the sun would not rise in the East.

Divine "Leave of Stay"

On many occasions during his last few years Master indicated that his time to go had long since passed; nevertheless, he had been able to secure divine permission for a further "leave of stay" on the earth. The childlike saint often talked with God in the form of the Divine Mother.

Mr. Cuaron, leader of the SRF center in Mexico City, wrote after

---

* Quoted from *Autobiography of a Yogi*, chapter 35.

Yoganandaji's passing: "Master said to me in various conversations: 'I am living on borrowed time. Divine Mother has asked me more than once to withdraw from this earth, as my time is up; and if I do not do it willingly, She will drag me away.' Master added that he was very grateful to Her, as several times She had granted Her consent to a continuation of his stay on earth in order to finish some important work."

"Greater Love Hath No Man"

In helping to lift the karmic load of disciples, a guru sometimes works out on his own body some of their karma.* In his compassionate love, Paramahansaji lightened the burden of many a disciple, and for this reason the great master suffered certain physical disabilities during the last two years of his life.† But he never complained. His angelic patience and cheerfulness were always an inspiration to those around him. He never said "no" to anyone in need of his spiritual help.

That his illness was a metaphysically induced one is proved by the fact that, whenever some occasion demanded his presence, he could always "take up his bed and walk." He granted many interviews to visitors who had no intimation that Master had left a sickbed to receive them, so well and radiant did he appear.

The "beginning of the end" may be placed as November 17, 1951. That was the date of death for his most advanced woman disciple, eighty-two-year-old Sister Gyanamata. Master conducted the funeral services for her at the SRF Hermitage in Encinitas. He told a disciple, "Now that Sister is gone, there is nothing that holds me here." In 1940 Yoganandaji had said to a little Encinitas resident who was in Gyana-mata's charge, "I shall not long outlive Sister."

After her funeral Master went to an SRF retreat in the desert, about 200 miles outside Los Angeles. He loved the desert, its spaciousness and silence.

---

* "Greater love hath no man than this, that a man lay down his life for his friends... I have called you friends; for all things that I have heard of my Father I have made known unto you." — *John* 15:13-16.

† See page 93.

Ambassador Sen, Yoganandaji, Mme. Sen, Mr. Bhandari, on the joyous occasion of His Excellency's visit, with his party from Washington, to SRF headquarters on March 4th—three days before Paramahansaji's *mahasamadhi*.

This many-windowed sun room was built on the third floor in 1934 to serve as a reception room. There, in the chair he occupied in this picture, Master granted interviews to thousands of visitors to the Mt. Washington Ashram.

"Whatever Divine Mother Wills!"

He returned to Los Angeles on December 18th in order to be in residence at SRF headquarters (Mount Washington Center) for the holiday season. Many times he referred to that Christmas as being perhaps his last. "Whatever Divine Mother wills!" he would say. On Christmas day he presided over a banquet at the headquarters. Sitting beside him was his beloved disciple Rajarsi Janakananda.* In the course of a talk on this occasion, Master said:

"Through suffering the consequences of wrong desires, man learns to choose right desires. When there is no desire there is no activity, and to be lazy is to be forsaken by God and man! The spiritual man works much harder than the worldly man, but what a great privilege it is to work for God! You must always be proud of it. Remember that renunciation of egotistical desires is the way to happiness."

Paramahansaji made a special effort to see that the holidays were a joyful time for all disciples and visitors. He granted many interviews. Though his health was not as good in Los Angeles as it had been in the desert, he would not spare himself. To the disciples he said, "I knew what would happen to me if I came in from the desert. But if I am making others happy, I am happy. This body means nothing to me. The sooner I leave it, the better." When devotees expressed their concern, he would only shake his head and say, "You do not know what Divine Mother is planning for me."

One evening, after he had been talking with visitors till very late, a disciple asked if his body weren't weary. "No, no!" Master exclaimed.

---

* Mr. J. J. Lynn, revered American disciple of Paramahansa Yogananda. Upon Master's *mahasamadhi* in March, Rajarsi became the president of Self-Realization Fellowship, which position he held until his death on February 20, 1955.

CAPTION FOR PICTURE ON OPPOSITE PAGE   →

Two monks of the Self-Realization Order are bowed in grief near the body of Paramahansa Yogananda, their sublime guru and truest friend.

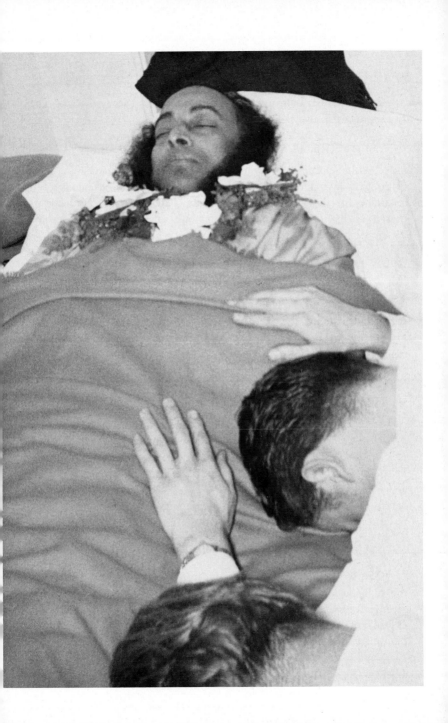

"I feel exhilarated. I am unmindful of the body and its limitations when I speak to others about God."

Ground Broken for First SRF Book House

On the morning of January 5th, Yoganandaji's birthday, a group of disciples met at the Hollywood Ashram Center for a ground-breaking ceremony for the first SRF Book House. Paramahansaji's birthday was chosen as the occasion for the ceremony to symbolize the devotees' appreciation of the inspiration of the Master's life.

Birthday Homage, Birthday Blessings

On the night of Master's birthday the disciples performed an ancient Indian ceremony honoring the guru. Chanting *Om Guru*, they passed before him in single file to receive his benediction. He sat in the chapel at Mt. Washington, wearing the gift of a beautiful flower garland. He lovingly embraced many of the monks, and gave a fervent blessing to each one of the 125 persons present, nearly all of whom were resident disciples at the Los Angeles, Hollywood, Pacific Palisades, Encinitas, and San Diego ashrams. After a banquet with a birthday cake, Paramahansaji gave a talk in which he said:

"The Lord has everything else He wants except our love. When we say, 'Thou art my Father, I am Thy child,' He responds with His great love. Jesus said: 'Thou hast hid these things from the wise and prudent, and hast revealed them unto babes.' * Before Him I am a babe, as I am before all who are kind to me. Your love and kindness to me I give to God.... I have presented all of you to Him as a bouquet of souls."

Last Day in Encinitas

Master left Los Angeles on January 10th for Encinitas. He spent the night at the SRF Hermitage there. On the following morning he greeted Rajarsi Janakananda, who exclaimed, "What a happy surprise!" "I had not planned to come to Encinitas," Paramahansaji replied, "but the pull of wanting to see you was too strong to resist." That afternoon

---

Matthew 11:25.

Photograph of Paramahansa Yogananda taken at his last birthday party, Self-Realization Fellowship headquarters, Los Angeles, January 5, 1952

Yoganandaji had dinner with Rajarsi, Dr. and Mrs. Lewis, and several other disciples. The group enjoyed "Calcutta croquettes," a potato entree whose recipe was originated by Master.

Later that day Yoganandaji saw for the last time the buildings and beautiful grounds of the Encinitas Ashram Center, founded by him in 1937. Admiring the gardens, he praised the work of Durga Mata, his disciple and an ashram resident since 1929, and at the ashram's public dining facility he greeted all friends and disciples present.

Yoganandaji returned on January 11th to the desert. There his health improved. He became, however, more and more reclusive, entering often into *samadhi* (superconscious trance). Sometimes he would ask a disciple to watch him, lest he fall from his meditation seat (as sometimes happens when a yogi's consciousness is withdrawn from the body).

He Seldom Slept, Seldom Cared to Eat

He slept little or not at all; such abstinence, however, had been his practice for many years. He increasingly did not care to eat. A few weeks before his passing he abandoned the simple diet he had followed for years. When he could be persuaded to eat at all, it had to be Hindu cookery. "I have a reason," he would say to the astonished disciples.

Master was a wonderful cook; as, indeed, he was skillful and out-standing in anything he undertook. During past years he had tried two or three times to make perfect *singharas*, an Indian potato-filled pastry. But the results had not satisfied him; they were, he said, "not just like those in the Indian bazaars." During February at the desert, however, he tried once more; the *singharas* came out exactly right. "Well," he said, "that is one more little desire fulfilled. There is just one more left."

Later the disciples understood that the "one more" little unfulfilled desire was for green coconut juice—and the Divine Mother arranged for the fulfillment of that wish on the day before he left his body.

Master often told his disciples stories of the great saints who, engrossed in the Infinite Romance, would see the fulfillment of all their innocent little wishes. St. Therese of Lisieux, for example, who loved snow, found that on the sunny day of her final vows, a light snow fell.

Immutability of Yogananda's Body

The following are extracts from a letter to Self-Realization Fellowship from Mr. Harry T. Rowe, Mortuary Director of Forest Lawn Memorial-Park. The full text of the letter appears on pages 121-124 inclusive.

"The absence of any visual signs of decay in the dead body of Paramahansa Yogananda offers the most extraordinary case in our experience... No physical disintegration was visible in his body even twenty days after death... No indication of mold was visible on his skin, and no visible desiccation (drying up) took place in the bodily tissues. This state of perfect preservation of a body is, so far as we know from mortuary annals, an unparalleled one...

"At the time of receiving Yogananda's body, the Mortuary personnel expected to observe, through the glass lid of the casket, the usual progressive signs of bodily decay. Our astonishment increased as day followed day without bringing any visible change in the body under observation. Yogananda's body was apparently in a phenomenal state of immutability . . . No odor of decay emanated from his body at any time . . . .

"The physical appearance of Yogananda on March 27th, just before the bronze cover of the casket was put into position, was the same as it had been on March 7th. He looked on March 27th as fresh and as unravaged by decay as he had looked on the night of his death. On March 27th there was no reason to say that his body had suffered any visible physical disintegration at all. For these reasons we state again that the case of Paramahansa Yogananda is unique in our experience."

The Grim Reaper, smiling at the loveliness of a true devotee of God, touched his body with no finger of decay. "The lips, which wore a slight smile, continuously retained their firmness," the Mortuary Director of Forest Lawn testified. "No odor of decay emanated from Yogananda's body at any time."

On January 28th Master went back to Los Angeles for a four-day stay. At Mt. Washington Center he enjoyed long talks on philosophy and the spiritual path with Professor David White of Macalester College, St. Paul, Minnesota. Yoganandaji returned on February 1st to the desert.

Paramahansaji felt a great joy and contentment in writing. At the desert he devoted most of his time to bringing forth from the inexhaustible ocean of his divine perceptions rare pearls of wisdom that would inspire all seekers of God. Hours slipped by like minutes. Many, many times it was daylight before he would think of stopping. "I dictate scriptural interpretations and letters all day," he wrote to a student, "with eyes closed to the world, but open always in heaven." He had to be reminded that it was time to do this or that; otherwise he would completely forget the body and its needs.

Only a night or two before he left the desert for the last time he was coaxed to stop working, and was about to go for his nightly walk, when he suddenly said, "Get out the typewriter. I am going to dictate something." The disciples demurred, urging him to rest, but he was adamant. Several hours' dictation followed, and the sky was beginning to lighten before he ended. Those who had been listening were spellbound by the beauty and depth of the scriptural explanation he had given, but expressed their concern that it had kept him so long. He replied very firmly, "If I hadn't done it tonight, it would never have been done."

Because Master could converse with rare insight on any subject,* many people thought he obtained his knowledge from books.

"You must be extremely well-read," a visitor observed one day.

"No," Yoganandaji replied, "I doubt that I have read twenty books in the past twenty years."

_____

* When he so desired, Master could instantly attune himself to the mind of any man (a yogic power mentioned in Patanjali's *Yoga Sutras,* III:19). That Yoganandaji could read one's thoughts is a fact well known to many of his close disciples. Like all great masters, he never flaunted this power, nor did he exercise it unless there was some particular reason to do so. Saints have no desire to pry into the thoughts of men—the secrets of God are too engrossing.

During the last weeks at the desert Master spoke with increasing emphasis about the unreality, the illusive substance, of the world. "See the mountain over there," he would say. "God has made us think that it is tons upon tons of dirt, standing there solidly. But it is nothing more than an illusory appearance, fabric of His dream. This mud-ball of earth whirling through space is held together only by the idea of it in the Creator's mind."

One night as he took his usual walk in the intense desert stillness, he looked off into the darkness and prayed to the Divine Mother to release him from his body. "My time is drawing near," he said later. "God has better things in store for us."

"Important Engagement" One of Many Hints

Several times during the last week of February Master gave the disciples around him a very broad hint (which none of them understood at the time) that he would pass on in March. He kept saying: "I have a very important engagement in March."

The disciples thought March to be important for other reasons. The Honorable M. R. Ahuja, Consul General of India at San Francisco, had arranged for India's Ambassador to America, Mr. Binay Ranjan Sen, to visit SRF centers in Los Angeles, Hollywood, and Pacific Palisades on March 4th. Mr. Ahuja wanted His Excellency to see the vast spiritual work that Paramahansaji set into motion in this country thirty-two years earlier. Ambassador Sen already knew of Yoganandaji's work in India, and had visited the Yogoda* headquarters there, "Yogoda Math," at Dakshineswar in Bengal.

Also, for March 7th the India Association of America, a Los Angeles organization, was planning a banquet at the Biltmore Hotel in honor of His Excellency and Madame Sen. Yoganandaji had been invited to be one of the speakers.

During the day on which Master first said, "I have a very important engagement in March," a disciple inquired, "Do you mean the day the Ambassador will visit you at Mt. Washington?"

---

* Self-Realization Fellowship is known in India as Yogoda Satsanga Society of India.

Tribute from W. Y. Evans-Wentz

Dr. Evans-Wentz, M.A., D.Litt., D.Sc., eminent
Orientalist, author of *Tibetan Yoga and
Secret Doctrines* (Oxford University Press)

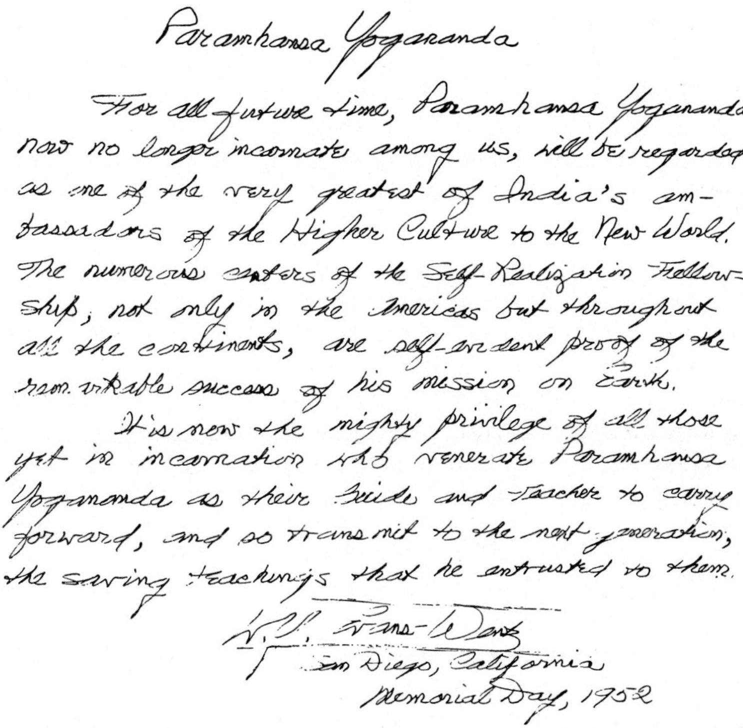

[handwritten letter]

Paramhansa Yogananda

For all future time, Paramhansa Yogananda, now no longer incarnate among us, will be regarded as one of the very greatest of India's ambassadors of the Higher Culture to the New World. The numerous centers of the Self-Realization Fellowship, not only in the Americas but throughout all the continents, are self-evident proof of the remarkable success of his mission on Earth.

It is now the mighty privilege of all those yet in incarnation who venerate Paramhansa Yogananda as their Guide and Teacher to carry forward, and so transmit to the next generation, the saving teachings that he entrusted to them.

W. Y. Evans-Wentz
San Diego, California
Memorial Day, 1952

"For all future time, Paramahansa Yogananda, now no longer incarnate among us, will be regarded as one of the very greatest of India's ambassadors of the Higher Culture to the New World. The numerous centers of Self-Realization Fellowship, not only in the Americas but throughout all the continents, are self-evident proof of the remarkable success of his mission on Earth.

"It is now the mighty privilege of all those yet in incarnation who venerate Paramahansa Yogananda as their Guide and Teacher to carry forward, and so transmit to the next generation, the saving teachings that he entrusted to them."

"No," he replied, "though that day is important, too."

"Do you mean the banquet on March 7th?" the disciple persisted.

Paramahansaji only looked away without reply. His demeanor was distant, withdrawn.

The passing in 1936 of Master's guru, Sri Yukteswarji, was on March 9th. Each time that Yoganandaji would refer to the coming festivity at the Biltmore Hotel he would say, "the banquet on March 9th." The disciples repeatedly reminded him that the correct date was the 7th. "Oh, yes, that's right," he would reply. But in his next reference to it he would again say, "the banquet on March 9th."

There were so many demands on his time and attention, it seemed that Paramahansaji could never get started before nightfall on his travels from one SRF ashram to another. He often spoke with mock disgust of this state of affairs, and when he prepared to return to Los Angeles for the welcoming festivities for the Ambassador, he was determined to leave the desert by daylight. He drove off at 3:30 p.m., on March 1st, and expressed his happiness again and again at seeing the varied desert scenes by the light of the sun.

Prepared Indian Delicacies for Ambassador

Master almost invariably cooked some part of the delicacies that were always prepared for guests. On Monday night, March 3rd, he directed and assisted with the making of Indian sweetmeats for the Ambassador and other guests. He said to one of the disciples who had been helping him in the kitchen, "I shall not be long here. It may be only a matter of days, even hours. Do you understand? even hours!"

The reader may wonder why, in view of the frequency and pointedness of Paramahansaji's remarks about leaving the body, the disciples indeed did not "understand." It was partly due to the fact that recently he had said such things so often — like the little boy crying "Wolf! Wolf!" — that their full significance was unrealized. It was as though each one's mind was clouded; the imminence of the Master's departure was never dreamed of. Truly it was difficult for the disciples to imagine the possibility of such a world calamity as Paramahansaji's passing, as

Master receives a box of *singharas* (Indian potato-filled pastry) which he presented to Mme. Sen. His joy in giving is evident. Mr. P. L. Bhandari of the Indian Embassy is at the right.

Paramahansa Yogananda with Mme. Sen, Ambassador Sen, and Consul General Ahuja upon their arrival March 4, 1952, at Self-Realization Fellowship international headquarters.

they watched him, active and joyful, greet the members of the Ambassador's party when they arrived on the morning of March 4th at the Mt. Washington Center.

Ambassador of India at SRF Headquarters

The party consisted of His Excellency and Mme. Sen, Embassy of India, Washington, D.C.; Consul General Ahuja; Mr. P. L. Bhandari, first secretary, Government of India Information Services, Washington, D.C.; Professor M. W. Sundaram, first secretary, Education Department, Government of India, Washington, D.C.; Dr. J. N. Sharma, former president of India Association of America; Mrs. Sharma; and Miss J. Campbell, the Ambassador's secretary.

The day was pleasant and sunny, though the breeze was cool. Yoganandaji greeted his visitors on the front-entrance porch, on which were displayed the flags of America and India. The traditional Hindu welcome was given: blowing of conchs, showering of rose petals, and the bestowal, by Master, of bright floral garlands. In response to His Excellency's greeting, Paramahansaji said with a childlike smile, "I am your humble servant."

Consul General's Appreciation of Master's Work

SRF disciples led the distinguished guests on a tour of the rooms on the first floor: the reception hall, chapel, print shop,* and large offices from which the SRF teachings are mailed to various parts of the world. In the print shop Mr. Ahuja greeted one of the monks who last year had demonstrated before the Consul General a number of the *asanas* (yoga postures) that are taught to the SRF residential students. Mr. Ahuja remarked to his party:

"In all India I never saw the *asanas* performed with more ease and less strain."

The group then joined Paramahansaji for an informal talk in the

---

*Owing to expansion of the Self-Realization work, the print shop was moved in 1956 to what is now the monks' office building and in 1971 to a still larger building near Mt. Washington.

third-floor reception room. Yoganandaji and the guests spoke of India and of the SRF ideals. Consul General Ahuja, who had come to know Master well during the preceding eighteen months, and who had traveled from San Francisco to be present at the dedication in 1951 of India Center, said appreciatively:

"Ambassadors may come and go, and consuls general may come and go; but you, Paramahansaji, are a true ambassador of India!"

Master's face filled with great sweetness and humility; he lowered his head, as he often did when anyone paid him a compliment, and smiled.

After receiving baskets of fruits and other gifts, the visitors went up on the roof of the sixty-room building. They were rewarded with a panoramic view of the city of Los Angeles. Master and all guests went downstairs to the lobby, and stood happily listening to a recording of India's national song, *Jana Gana Mana.*

Ambassador Visits Hollywood Temple

The party was going to the Self-Realization Center in Hollywood for lunch. The cars were waiting in the driveway. His Excellency asked Yoganandaji where he wished to be seated. "Wherever you place me," Master said. Just before Mr. Ahuja stepped into the automobile, he turned to one of the Indians and asked, "Do you see the wonderful organization and cooperation and devotion here?"

The guests visited the charming Hollywood Temple before entering the adjoining India Hall. The Ambassador said he was much impressed by the dignity and beauty of the building and the picturesque grounds. Lunch was served about 1:30 p.m. in the library of India Hall. Master and his guests enjoyed an all-Indian meal of cauliflower curry with *channa* (cheese of fresh curdled milk), Calcutta croquettes (potato balls), lentil *dal* (thick soup with spices), *singharas* (potato-filled pastry), fried eggplant, *luchis* (puffed-up Indian bread), chutney, and rice. A fresh lime drink was served, and four Indian desserts — mango paste and three sweetmeats (*rasagulla, sandesh, channa bora*), all made from *channa* and flavored with imported oil-of-*keora.*

AMBASSADOR'S PARTY WITH YOGANANDAJI AT MT. WASHINGTON CENTER

(*Left to right*) Consul General Ahuja, Mr. Dick Haymes, Miss Jessie Campbell, Ambassador Sen, and Yoganandaji, at SRF headquarters, March 4, 1952

Ambassador and Party Visit SRF Lake Shrine

The Ambassador's party departed at 3 p.m. to keep another appointment. In the late afternoon, however, His Excellency and Mme. Sen,
Mr. Ahuja, Mr. Bhandari, and Professor Sundaram drove out to Pacific
Palisades for an hour's visit at SRF Lake Shrine. Rev. Mr. Stanley, with
Brahmachari Adolph, welcomed the party, and presented Mme. Sen
with a garland of red and white camellias. The guests were escorted
around the lovely two-acre lake and saw the houseboat, the outdoor
Golden Lotus Temple, the windmill house and its quiet chapel, the water-
wheel house (in which Yogananda Museum is now located), and the World
Peace Memorial containing a portion of Mahatma Gandhi's ashes. At the
end of the tour Mr. Stanley asked the Ambassador if he weren't tired.

"No," replied His Excellency, "this day has been one I shall always
remember." He added, "This is a beautiful spot. I hope someday to see it
with Paramahansaji."

Ambassador Sen wrote the following letter to Yoganandaji on
March 5th:

Dear Paramahansaji:

*It is very hard for me to express my appreciation for the hospitality
and friendliness we received when we visited Mount Washington yester-
day. It was most interesting and enlightening to me to see the wonderful
work you are doing in this part of the world, and I was very grateful
for the opportunity to know about this.*

*On behalf of my whole party may I thank you and wish you all
that is best in your very fine work in interpreting India and Indian
philosophy to the people of this country.*

Very sincerely,
B. R. SEN
Ambassador of India

After the Ambassador's party left India Hall, about 3 p.m. (March
4th), Yoganandaji remained there until eight o'clock. It was his first
visit in six months to this, his latest SRF foundation. He chatted with

Dick Haymes; Eunice Richardson, an Encinitas disciple; her mother, Mrs. T. Ratliff; and Meera Mata, the disciple in charge of the Hollywood Ashram Center.

"You must love and serve one another, as you have served me. I am the servant of all," Master said at the end of a talk about the Self-Realization work.

Yoganandaji later invited Meera Mata to go to the banquet on March 7th at the Biltmore Hotel. "Master," she inquired, "do you really want me to go?"

"Why do you ask?" he answered. "You must go. All eyes will be upon you."

(Meera Mata, clad in a gold-embroidered silk sari, attended the banquet. After Master sank to the floor at the conclusion of his speech, many weeping Self-Realization Fellowship students who had been sitting in various parts of the large room made their way in panic to Meera Ma's table. It was directly in front of Paramahansaji's place at the long speaker's table. One more prediction was thus fulfilled.)

At Hollywood Ashram Center that Tuesday Master granted interviews to various disciples.

The picture at left was taken at SRF India Hall, Hollywood, March 4th, when Paramahansaji (*in background, at head of table*) was host at a luncheon for Ambassador and Mme. Sen and their party.

(*Right*) Yoganandaji and disciples at lunch — the last meal taken by Master at SRF Lake Shrine, Pacific Palisades, March 6th.

While he was talking with one of them — a Mexican — he told a few stories about his vacation in Mexico. (It was in 1929; he was received at the palace in the capital by the President of Mexico, and visited Lake Chapala, Xochimilco, and other beautiful spots.) In a gay mood, Paramahansaji recounted how he had managed fairly well to pass three months in Mexico with a vocabulary of only a dozen Spanish words. "The people are very kind and lovable," he observed. He added, laughing, "They were constantly saying to me, 'Si, si, Senor!' and I was looking everywhere!"

In the evening Master walked down the hallway between the library and the dining room. Returning to the group, he said slowly: "I have walked the halls of India Center* at last." (On his previous visits to the charming building, which was erected in 1950-1951 under his supervision, he had not been well enough to do much walking.)

A Last Supper With His Disciples

Master spent the following day, Wednesday, March 5th, in seclusion in his third-floor apartment in the Mt. Washington Center. He told Rev. M. W. Lewis and Mrs. Lewis and a small group of sisters of the SRF Order that he was planning a dinner for them at five o'clock. Ordinarily such meals were quite informal. This Wednesday, however, a certain ceremonious atmosphere prevailed. Paramahansaji had a table set up in his small sitting room, and was very particular about the seating arrangements and other details. He asked that plates be taken to two disciples who could not be invited for lack of space.

Indian dishes, prepared at Master's direction in his small kitchen, were served: rice, cauliflower curry, *singharas,* fried *channa, luchis,* Indian sweetmeats, and a fresh lime drink. This was sumptuous fare indeed for the disciples, who were used to a very simple diet.

During the meal all the devotees noticed how quiet and thoughtful Yoganandaji was. Before dinner ended the telephone rang in an adjoining room. A disciple took the call, which came from Mr. J. Oliver Black in Detroit. She answered Mr. Black's questions and was about to hang up

---

* Now known as India Hall.

the receiver when Master asked: "Is he going to call again?" "No, Sir," she replied. "Then I had better talk with him. I may not have another chance," Paramahansaji remarked as he rose from his chair.

A few hours before Sister Gyanamata's death on November 17, 1951, Yoganandaji gave a dinner in Encinitas for a number of devotees. Later he said: "The disciples didn't know why I held that dinner. It was in honor of Sister. I knew she was going. It is a custom in India, when great souls leave this earth, to celebrate with a banquet their release in God."

Readers of *Autobiography of a Yogi* (chapter 27) will remember the story of the farewell feast given by Swami Pranabananda, the "saint with two bodies." After he and his disciples had fed 2000 persons, the

Ambassador Sen and Yoganandaji in discussion at Self-Realization Fellowship headquarters, Los Angeles, March 4, 1952

great master gave a talk on the Infinite and then consciously gave up his body.

Lord Jesus, too, just before his passing, observed the Oriental custom when he sent Peter and John to prepare, for him and the twelve disciples, a Last Supper.*

The devotees who were with Paramahansaji on the evening of March 5th understood later that, in honor of his approaching *mahasamadhi,* he too had arranged a Last Supper.

Breakfast with Ambassador Sen

His Excellency had invited Yoganandaji to attend a breakfast that he was giving for about thirty-five members of the Indian community in southern California. Master therefore set out for the breakfast at the Hotel Ambassador in Los Angeles about 8 a.m. on Thursday, March 6th. A disciple who was visiting SRF headquarters for a few days, accompanied Paramahansaji on the early drive. He writes:

"I joined Master as he was walking toward his car. He cautioned the disciples to use special care in lifting gifts of chutney and Indian sweetmeats, made by him and several disciples, that he was taking to Ambassador Sen and Consul General Ahuja. Master was very joyous on the way. He told a few stories about his early years in this country: his first transcontinental lecture tour, in 1924, by automobile, when three young men accompanied him; his visit to inspiring Pikes Peak near Denver; his experiences with different makes of autos.

"He was bubbling over with divine love. The vibrations of peace and bliss coming from him were overwhelming. He took my hand in his, and said: 'If you all work together with love, harmony, kindness, and humility, the work will sweep the world.' He was referring, of course, to the SRF teachings of self-liberation through *Kriya Yoga.*

"Master told Cliff, who was driving, and me that we might have our breakfast in the Ambassador Hotel Coffee Shop while he kept his appointment with His Excellency. Giving us some money, he inquired,

* *Luke* 22:7-14.

Tribute from Mme. Galli-Curci

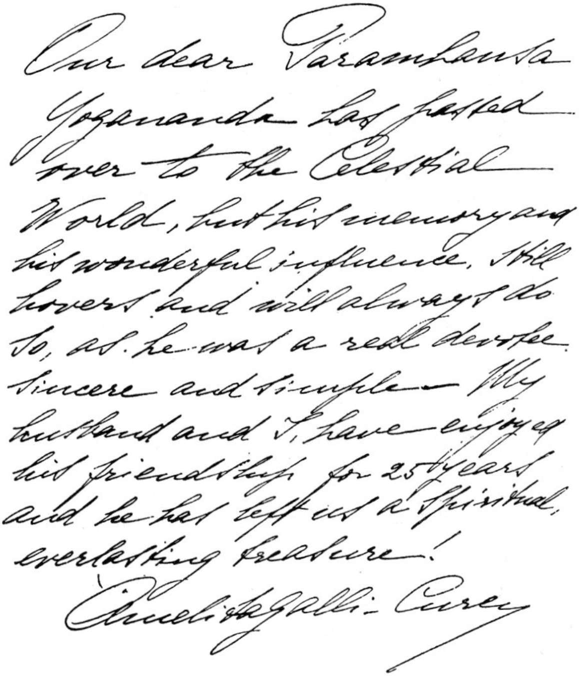
Our dear Paramhansa
Yogananda has passed
over to the Celestial
World, but his memory and
his wonderful influence, still
hovers and will always do
so, as he was a real devotee
sincere and simple — My
husband and I, have enjoyed
his friendship for 25 years
and he has left us a spiritual,
everlasting treasure!
Amelita Galli-Curci

"Our dear Paramahansa Yogananda has passed over to the Celestial World, but his memory and his wonderful influence still hovers and will always do so, as he was a real devotee, sincere and simple. My husband and I have enjoyed his friendship for twenty-five years; and he has left us a spiritual, everlasting treasure."

'Are you sure this is sufficient? I want you both to eat enough.' We assured him we had plenty of money for breakfast, but he insisted on giving us more.

"Master began a slow walk through the beautiful hotel, with Cliff and me helping him, as walking was difficult for him. Mr. Bhandari, one of His Excellency's party from Washington, met us halfway and led Master to the private breakfast room. The Ambassador and the Consul General were waiting courteously at the door, not wanting to enter the room until after Master had arrived.

"After our own meal Cliff and I returned to the breakfast room, to find Master just coming out, with Mr. Bhandari at his side. After walking a little way through the hotel, we all stopped in front of a large display of anthuriums, the glossy flowers from Hawaii. Master smiled and remarked how beautiful they were. I said, 'Sir, you are walking too much; may I please order a chair and push you?' He shook his head, but I pleaded again. He looked at me with a piercing gaze and said, 'Mind can do anything.' Master and Mr. Bhandari carried on a lively discussion about India until we reached the car.

Last Visit to SRF Lake Shrine

"We then drove out to SRF Lake Shrine in Pacific Palisades, to see how the repair work was coming along after the recent damaging rains. It was Master's first visit in six months to the Shrine. He greeted everyone, expressing pleasure in the work that was being done. We took him around the lake. 'I want to see it all,' he said, and his observant eyes didn't miss a single detail along the way. We stopped often so that he could get a good look at the different plants, shrubs, and trees.

"We walked up the gangplank to the Mississippi houseboat. Master sat in the living room and talked at some length with the Lake Shrine disciples who were happily grouped around him. We had become engrossed in a discussion of the grave world situation when Master said, 'It is all God's play,' and gave a talk on cosmic delusion and how the Lord uses different actors on the stage of time to portray certain parts.

"Stanley announced that lunch was ready, so we left the houseboat. As we walked along, Master continually commented on articles to be

Paramahansaji greets the Ambassador and his party upon their arrival at Self-Realization Fellowship headquarters, Los Angeles. *(From left)* Mme. Sen, His Excellency Mr. Sen, Consul General Ahuja.

repaired or repainted, and about new things to be added to the grounds.

"A moment later we were going down an incline and walking a little more rapidly than before. Two of us hurried Master forward. He said, 'Be careful. Food you will always have, but me you will not always have with you.'

"We soon arrived at the windmill house for lunch. Master enjoyed it, and told us little stories about food, and that the 'proper-eatarian' diet is the best. 'There are so many good meat substitutes,' he remarked.

"Afterward Master sat before the organ and played several of his chants and other Indian music. Over and over he sang the ancient Bengali chant for which Tagore wrote the words: 'In my house with Thine own hands light the lamp of Thy love . . . Change my darkness to Thy light, change my darkness to Thy light.' He and the disciples chanted this repeatedly, and our hearts were filled with rapture. A real devotee of God was singing to the Divine Mother, and we felt his love and devotion and the bliss flowing from his hallowed temple. He played the organ for at least an hour, perhaps longer. Perspiration was streaming down his face; his eyes were radiant with joy.

"We went outside by the lake's edge, and Stanley called the ducks. Master threw bread and corn to them. We discussed the right spot in which to place one of the art treasures of Self-Realization Fellowship —a large reproduction in mother-of-pearl of Christ with his disciples at the Last Supper.*

"Little did any of us realize, as we chatted about the best location for the picture, that at the windmill house we had just had the Last Supper that Master was to eat at an ashram with his young men disciples.

"Master, Cliff, and I drove off about 4:45 p.m., having visited the Lake Shrine for nearly six hours. As soon as we entered the car, Master became inwardly withdrawn. He was grave and silent for the most part —the opposite of his morning mood.

"When we arrived at the driveway of SRF headquarters, Master

---

* This beautiful carved bas-relief, which was made in Europe by Gabriel Afana, was exhibited in 1933 at the Chicago World's Fair. It is now at SRF headquarters.

said, 'Oh, are we here already? Let us go back and around. I want to get a good view of the building. I will direct you.' Cliff drove down San Rafael Avenue to a spot where, across a canyon of shrubbery, the Mt. Washington headquarters could be seen to good advantage, standing bold against the sky. The sun had nearly set. The building looked magnificent and very white. Master said, 'The new paint job is wonderful. It was needed.' He told me how the SRF students had done it themselves and saved tremendous expense. Then he fell into a reverie and mused, with a sigh, 'It looks just like a castle.' 'It is our castle, Sir,' Cliff said. Master smiled and replied, 'Yes, a castle for men and women of God.' Then he looked at the Mt. Washington Center for a long time in silence.

"We drove back to the headquarters, where a number of the monks, just finished with their period of exercise on the tennis court, were waiting to greet Master. He gave a wonderful talk about the spiritual

(*Left*) Master throws bread to the fish in the beautiful two-acre lake, SRF Lake Shrine, Pacific Palisades, March 6, 1952.

(*Right*) Yoganandaji plays the organ in the chapel. This was his last *sankirtan* (gathering of devotees to sing God's praises); he played and sang with joy for more than an hour.

path, and how to keep steadfast on it, even after he would depart. I became a little sad, thinking that some distant day his physical presence would be gone; but the tremendous zeal and dynamic enthusiasm that now emanated from him seemed reassuring. I had no inkling that he would be leaving the earth so soon. I realize now that he was preparing us for it. I did not then connect all his remarks as I did later, after he had gone.

"He touched on many topics, and counseled us to be more grave, but cheerful. 'Don't waste time,' he said. 'No one else can give you the desire for God; you must cultivate that yourself. The Lord Himself can't give it to you. Learn to want Him. Don't intellectualize and rationalize, and never doubt that God will come to you. When duties are done, give your time to meditation and to experiencing inwardly the Divine Power.

" 'Don't sleep a great deal. Sleep is enjoyable because it is an unconscious contact with God. But you should spend more time in meditation. That is the state beyond sleep, in which you are consciously aware of the blissful presence of the Lord.

" 'Don't joke all the time with each other. Be happy and cheerful inside. Why dissipate in useless talk the perceptions you have gained? Words are like bullets; when you spend their force in idle conversation, your supply of inner ammunition is wasted. Your consciousness is like a milk pail: when you fill it with the peace of meditation you ought to keep it that way. Joking is often false fun that drives holes in the sides of your bucket and allows all the milk of your peace to run out.

The Three Greatest Delusions

" 'Wine, sex, and money — these are the three greatest delusions. Some men are weak, but what of that? If they will meditate they will get a sense of comparison with something better, and will automatically forsake their bad habits. You can conquer these delusions only by experience of Reality. Sex seems attractive, but if you would learn the real spiritual union, how much more wonderful you would find it!

" 'Don't waste time on distractions, reading a great deal, and so on. Reading is good, if it is truly instructive. But when reading takes the place of meditation, then it is spiritually worthless. Read a little for inspiration, but spend most of your time in meditation and silence. Just think: every week 100 books are printed. You couldn't read all of them if you wanted to. The most brilliant person in the world can learn only the merest fraction of what there is to be known about the world around us. The scientist knows much, but he can't explain how even a leaf was made. Why only chew other people's ideas by reading all the time? I always say, "If you read one hour, then write two hours, think three hours, and meditate all the time." No matter how intensely busy the organization keeps me, I always practice *Kriya Yoga* and meditate.

"'Develop your powers of devotion to God. If you pick up even a straw and give it to God, He will accept your devotion. And the respect that you give to me, give to one another. Be kind to one another, just as you have been kind to me. To see evil in someone is to desecrate him, because the Lord is behind even the evil. To see good in others is to see God there.

"'If others fool away their time, *you* be lost in God. You will go ahead. Prepare yourself. This work will spread all over the world. Love people with divine love and be only with those that love the Lord. Let your example change others' lives. Reform yourself and you will reform thousands.

"'Egotism is the hardest thing to overcome. When people say good things about you, give the credit to God. Love Him. Cry for Him. What does anything matter, so long as you find Him? Throw yourself into God, be filled with His love and joy. If you could feel even a little bit of the bliss I know, you would understand the magnitude of what you are missing.'

"Master got out of the car at the side entrance to the headquarters building, and began walking through the ground-floor hallway to the elevator. On the way, he spied a crate in a corner. 'What's in that box?' he cried at once. A disciple opened it, informing Master that it had been sent from Florida by air express by an SRF student, Mr. George, and that it had arrived at the Mt. Washington headquarters that very afternoon. The box was filled with green coconuts.

"'Divine Mother told me in the car that I would find something

Paramahansa Yogananda, world teacher of yoga ("union" of man with God), demonstrated its efficacy not only in life but in death. For weeks after his departure his face shone with the divine luster of incorruptibility.

for me in the house here,' Master said. 'This is what She meant. I wrote to George a long time ago, asking him if there are any green coconuts in Florida. He didn't reply and I forgot all about it. But Divine Mother didn't forget! George will be much blessed for having sent these.'

"The top of the largest coconut was chopped off. Master gave a little shout. 'Now for the juice!' He drank it with relish, and shared the meat with all the disciples around him. He went on. 'One coconut is a big meal, very healthful. This is the first time I have had green coconut juice since I returned to America from my trip to India sixteen years ago.'

"Though Master was chuckling merrily, the monks, very strangely, were not smiling with him. We sensed a certain unreality in the atmosphere; was Master playing a part for our benefit? Though he spoke of material things, around him was an air of complete detachment.

"He continued, 'I am just fulfilling these last little desires. If you have something, you enjoy it as a gift from God; if you don't have it, you don't mind.' He started toward the elevator, saying as he went, 'I have a big day tomorrow.' He added—using a popular American phrase that sounded casual but was indeed not so—'Wish me luck.' "

On the third floor Master met a few devotees near the elevator. They told him a crate from Florida had come that afternoon for him by air express. "Yes, I know," he replied. "My last little desire has been fulfilled. I wanted to drink coconut milk, just as I used to in India, once more * before I go."

This hint was broad enough, yet the disciples did not grasp its meaning. Yoganandaji wrote in his *Autobiography* that Babaji possesses a power by which he can prevent any specific thought from arising in a person's mind. The devotees now believe that Paramahansaji exercised that same power in connection with their own minds, lest they be thrown into unbearable grief at a forewarning of his imminent departure.

---

* "But these things have I told you, that when the time shall come, you may remember that I told you of them. And these things I said not unto you at the beginning, because I was with you. But now I go my way to Him that sent me." —*John* 16:4-5.

"He Asked me to Pray"

Sraddha Mata, a disciple of Master's for thirty-nine years, has written her recollections of Thursday, March 6th—the last night that Yoganandaji spent with his disciples at SRF headquarters. She writes: "His mood that evening was gentle and happy and tender toward us all. In spite of the long, strenuous day, his body showed no signs of fatigue — a fact we noticed immediately, as we had been anxious about him. We asked him to tell us something about the breakfast party given that morning by Ambassador Sen. For a while he made no reply to our questions; then, his face lit by an ecstatic smile, he said simply: 'He asked me to pray!'

"To my knowledge that is the only reference he made to the breakfast gathering. He was always so happy when any social occasion gave him the opportunity to pray, to speak of God and draw men's attention to the spiritual realities; for this was his mission in life and his only reason for attending public and social functions at any time. He was grateful and deeply touched that His Excellency had given him this opportunity.

"Master asked for something to eat. I brought him a little Indian food; he divided some of it into portions and told me to take them to a few disciples on the third floor. Master always liked to hear the ten o'clock news broadcast, and asked for it on this night also. When it was over, he walked down the long third-floor hall to the little porch at the end. He stopped on the way for a minute, sitting in the chair under Sri Yukteswarji's picture (a large embroidered one, made of colored yarn).

"On the porch he did the SRF energization exercises. Unfailingly he exercised, and walked as much as possible. He cautioned us all that we must follow his teachings in this respect, as in all others, in order to keep our health for the work we must do."

Friday — "Destiny Day"

Another devotee recalls a few incidents of the following day — Friday, March 7th, the Day of Destiny not only for the incomparable Master but for all his disciples. She writes:

"On the morning of the banquet, Master said, under his breath,

'I have a very important engagement in March.' I reminded him, 'This is March, Sir,' and he said, 'Yes, it is.' 'What engagement do you have that is so very important, Sir?' I went on. 'Is it the one with the Ambassador tonight?' 'No,' he replied, 'this one is *very* important.' I questioned the other disciples, but no one knew of any engagement except the banquet for the Ambassador that evening."

Awakener of Hearts

Sri Daya Mata, Yoganandaji's disciple since 1931,* gives her recollections of his last day at headquarters: "Throughout the long day of March 7th, Master was very quiet, asking that no one speak in his presence, and that those in adjoining rooms tiptoe softly about their work. Through the years the devotees had come to recognize this request as one that indicated that his consciousness was inwardly withdrawn to an even greater extent than usual. Often that day the disciples saw his eyes turn upward to the spiritual-eye center in the forehead. When he spoke at all, it was in terms of great affection, appreciation, and kindness.

"Most noticeable of all was the influence, felt by everyone who entered his sitting room, of the vibrations of intense divine love that emanated from him. The disciples felt as though they were standing in the presence of the Great Mother Herself. She had taken complete possession of him, it seemed, and was using him as a perfect channel to send out waves of love to all creation.

"His prayer, the one he quoted most often, is: 'May Thy love shine forever on the sanctuary of my devotion, and may I be able to awaken Thy love in all hearts.' To the very end, the Mother fulfilled Master's ardent desire."

Deep and Holy Quiet

Sraddha Mata has written the following account of March 7th: "On this morning he sent for me about 10 a.m. My first impression as I entered his room was of an unusually deep and holy quiet, pervaded

---

*Sri Daya Mata has served as president of Self-Realization Fellowship/Yogoda Sat-Satsanga Society of India since 1955.

Mme. Sen and Paramahansa Yogananda, at a banquet held in honor of Mr. Binay R. Sen, Ambassador of India, Biltmore Hotel, Los Angeles, March 7, 1952. Photograph taken an hour before Yoganandaji's passing.

with *Aum* vibration. He was meditating. I sat down and meditated with him — blessed privilege! — for ten minutes.

"He gave me some instructions about the trip to the Biltmore Hotel. A suite of two rooms had been engaged there for him, because it was his plan to go early and rest until it was time to take his place at the speakers' table in the banquet room of the hotel.

"An incident occurred that showed how Divine Mother granted Master's little wishes. He had asked me to be sure to get possession of the key to his hotel suite so he would not be delayed in reaching it. But the desk clerk had refused permission for the key to be taken away. However, Shyama Mata (Sri Daya Mata's mother) went to the hotel on Friday afternoon to register for Master and to see the suite. The room attendant, she discovered, was a man who had long wanted to meet Master and was eager to be of service to him. He readily granted permission for the key, then in the door lock, to be carried off.

"At Mt. Washington that afternoon I packed an overnight bag for Master in case he decided to remain all night at the hotel, since the banquet and reception would not be over until late. I then went to my room. Returning to Master's sitting room about 3:30 p.m., I opened the door quietly. A feeling of shock or apprehension came over me, for Master was lying in his large reclining chair in a position of such relaxation as to suggest the stillness of death. This was the thought that fled across my mind. I softly spoke a word of greeting. Master opened his eyes a little, smiled, and touched my forehead with his blessed little hand. About four o'clock he went downstairs and, after a talk with several devotees, smilingly entered his car. The rain had stopped earlier, but the day was still misty. Nevertheless, as Master left the Mt. Washington Ashram, the sun came out briefly. It was the hour of heavy traffic; we did not reach the Biltmore until nearly 5 p.m. Having the room key with him enabled Master to go directly to his suite. He had been silent for the most part during the drive; the deep quiet still prevailed in his hotel room. I made one or two remarks, but he only replied: 'Do not disturb my thoughts. My thoughts must not be disturbed.' He spoke very softly and slowly, conveying to me a sense of his remoteness. I seated myself to wait till he was ready to go downstairs.

"As I look back over this day I see a singular significance in many apparently trifling happenings, all of which struck me with a queer little shock at the time, for fleeting seconds, as though it were all a picture; something 'crystallized in time' were the words that later came to my mind."

Eyes That Saw God

"On the last day," according to another disciple, "Master sat in his chair with his eyes half-closed almost the entire day, wanting no talking around him, and no one to speak until he spoke. He appeared to be completely withdrawn from everything, as though a veil were forming between him and the mundane world.

"In his hotel suite that evening, I noticed a strange look in his eyes, and asked him questions, hoping to receive satisfaction that all was well. But he evaded the questions many times. Looking back now, I realize that he knew he was soon to leave the body, for his eyes were veiled with a faraway look that I had never seen in them before. I asked him if he planned to remain at the hotel all night, and he replied, 'I won't be staying here tonight.'"

Another disciple recalls that, just before Yoganandaji entered his car at the headquarters, he spoke to various monks and nuns, reminding them of the prime importance of their spiritual progress. Then he said: "Imagine! I have a room at the Biltmore. I am going back to where it all started."

(He was referring to his early days in Los Angeles, when he lived for many months at the Biltmore Hotel. From his room there, in 1925, he was able to look out of his window and see the many thousands of people queued around the block on each night that he was scheduled to lecture at the nearby Philharmonic Auditorium. "It looks like Times Square in New York during the rush hour," one Los Angeles reporter wrote at the time. One evening in 1925 Master gazed down from his room at the waiting crowds near the Philharmonic, and said to a disciple: "Babaji told me it would be like this.")

The banquet at the Biltmore in 1952 was scheduled to start about seven p.m. Shortly before that time two friends went to Paramahansaji's

At this, his Last Supper, Yoganandaji is symbolically seated between East and West. Mme. Sen, wife of the Ambassador of India, is a Bengali; Mrs. Sharma, wife of Dr. J. N. Sharma, is an Englishwoman.

room to escort him downstairs.

The trio entered the banquet hall — the Music Room of the Biltmore — a few minutes after seven o'clock. Yoganandaji was directed to his seat at the speakers' table. On his right was Mme. Sen, a Bengali, wife of the Ambassador of India; on his left was Mrs. Sharma, an English-woman, wife of Dr. J. N. Sharma of Los Angeles. On this, the Last Supper of all, Master was thus symbolically placed between East and West.

About 240 guests were present, including thirty-five SRF students from Los Angeles and nearby cities. Twenty persons were seated at the speakers' table, long and comparatively narrow, which was placed on a platform that elevated the guests of honor above the floor level. The majority of the guests sat at circular tables. To accommodate those for whom no seats were available in the Music Room, additional tables were set up in an anteroom.

Sri Daya Mata and Ananda Mata (who, with their mother, the late Shyama Mata, have been resident disciples in Paramahansaji's ashram for more than forty years) were present at the banquet. They had made reservations for seats directly in front of Master's place at the speakers' table. Through some error their seats were given to other persons. Daya Mata, Ananda Mata, and Sraddha Mata therefore sought out a table in the anteroom.

Yoganandaji looked at the tables in front of him and did not see the three disciples. He beckoned to Mr. Frederick, who was seated two tables away, and inquired if they were present. Mr. Frederick replied, "Yes, Sir," and unobtrusively pointed them out to Master as they stood in the distant doorway of the anteroom.

"An expression of deep kindness, of very great blessing, then came over his face," Mr. Frederick recounted later. The beloved Master, who never forgot any goodness shown him, thus remembered, by his look of farewell benediction, to thank three disciples who had long served him faithfully.

Mr. Frederick, who generally photographed Master and his guests at any SRF gathering, had been instructed by Yoganandaji not to take any pictures at the Biltmore. Probably Master had made that request

Tribute from Swami Sivananda

The Divine Life Society
Rishikesh, Himalayas, India

25th March, 1952

"He is eternal, all-pervading, stable, immovable, and ancient.

"A rare gem of inestimable value, the like of whom the world is yet to witness, H.H. Sri Paramahansa Yogananda has been an ideal representative of the ancient sages and seers, the glory of India.

"He has rendered yeoman service in the field of spirituality. He has greatly contributed towards the spiritual progress of all by setting in action the spiritual dynamo that is latent in men. Sri Yogananda has made it possible for all God's children to taste the nectar that flows in abundance from the eternal source, the *Vedas* and the *Upanishads.*

"Today the world centers of Self-Realization Fellowship represent Paramahansa Yogananda in action. They will multiply themselves, making a closely woven magnetic net of spirituality that will shower peace and bliss on the world.

"*Bhajan, sankirtan,* and special prayers were conducted here for the peace and bliss of the departed soul.

"May Self-Realization Fellowship prosper well, shedding divine light all over the world!"

SIVANANDA

because the banquet was sponsored not by Self-Realization Fellowship but by the India Association of America. Unfailingly, in every situation that arose in daily life, Paramahansaji manifested an exquisite sense of propriety and courtesy.

The Master Playwright

Insignia of the handiwork of the Master Playwright may be detected in all the details in the drama of Yoganandaji's passing. To SRF disciples it seems no accident that a commercial photographer was present at the banquet and took many beautiful pictures of the great guru during his last hours on earth.

The cameraman, Mr. Arthur Say, who also photographed Ambassador Sen and other celebrities, had never met Paramahansaji before March 7th. The young man had long been interested in India, however, and spent several years there during World War II. He attended the banquet as a guest of Mr. Ram Bagai, former president of the Hollywood Foreign Correspondents' Association. "When I received a printed invitation from the India Association," Mr. Say later told the editor of *Self-Realization Magazine*, "I felt a strong inclination to accept it. The young lady who had planned to accompany me decided at the last minute not to go, but I was determined to be present." He added, "I have never regretted it when I have obeyed the urgings of the still small voice within."

Guests at the dinner were given their choice of several courses. Master was served fruit salad, a vegetable plate, and strawberry parfait. But he ate very little. Several disciples who were seated at nearby tables observed that their guru scarcely touched his food. He was attentive, however, to his dinner companions, and conversed affably with Mme. Sen and Mrs. Sharma. Halfway through the meal he summoned Mr. Frederick to fetch some butter for the Ambassador's wife.

Mrs. Sharma later stated: "Paramahansaji was very kind and thoughtful. He said to me once or twice: 'Please excuse my talking in Bengali with Madame Sen. We are having a wonderful time chatting in our mother tongue!' Then the three of us would talk together for a while in English.

"Paramahansaji was perspiring about the face,* but seemed happy and composed. He was in good health, apparently, and presented no signs of being tired, faint, or in pain."

* This condition was not unusual. For many years Yoganandaji had perspired freely, chiefly around the head and neck. Perspiration was especially profuse when he was at prayer or invoking the Lord's aid for the physical or mental healing of others. Such exudation, odorless in most cases but sometimes possessing a faint flowerlike fragrance, is a characteristic feature of the state of *samadhi* or God-union. (*Publisher's Note*)

Mrs. Bhagat Singh Thind presents Mme. Sen with an orchid. Yoganandaji, his gaze withdrawn, is serious, yet sweet and calm. Photograph taken about half an hour before his passing.

She added, "We talked of deep things — of mankind, and philosophies, and the Infinite God. The last words Paramahansaji said to me were these: 'Always remember: life has its beautiful roses and also its thorns; and we must accept both.'"

We may perhaps surmise from these final words to Mrs. Sharma that Yoganandaji was attempting to soften slightly the shock that the gracious lady was soon to feel at his passing.

After dinner Miss Singh rendered stanzas of India's national anthem. Congressman D. S. Saund, president (at that time) of the India Association, who presided over the gathering as chairman, then asked Dr. Sharma to introduce to the audience the two guests of honor, Ambassador and Mme. Sen, and others at the speakers' table.

Mrs. Bhagat Singh Thind, president of The American Wives of India, presented an orchid to Mme. Sen, who stood smilingly near the speakers' stand while the flower was pinned on the sheer Indian shawl draped over her beautiful sari.

Dr. Saund spoke briefly on the necessity for unity between East and West. Mr. John Anson Ford, member of the Los Angeles County Board of Supervisors, delivered an eloquent address in which he said that, rich though young America is in material resources, it yet can greatly benefit by open-mindedness to the wisdom flowing from India's ancient culture.

Master Showed No Signs of Illness

Paramahansaji was always an ideal guest, considerate and appreciative, whether in a private home or at a public function. But then, was there *any* way in which Master failed to display the beauty of a life that is attuned to the Divine Will?

Tonight at the banquet, however, Yoganandaji did not gaze about him with his usual heart-warming smile, nor did he laugh at any of the amusing anecdotes in the various speeches. He was not stern, and only occasionally grave, but an aura of strangeness surrounded him that was quickly detected by all his disciples at nearby tables.

After the talk by Mr. Ford, Dr. Saund introduced Colonel Steinberg. He spoke with fervor of Self-Realization Fellowship and its influence

Pope's Pronouncements

The Vatican last week made important pronouncements on three subjects:

¶ In the kind of letter seldom sent to any but a Catholic country, Pope Pius XII sent a message to the Russian people. Reminding them of past ties with Rome, he prayed "that the Christian faith, which is the honor and support of human society, may be strengthened and increased among the peoples of Russia, and that all the wiles of the enemies of religion, all their errors and their deceptive artifices may be driven far off from you." This announcement, widely broadcast by the Vatican radio, was the Pope's way of saying that the church's attack on Communism is moral, not political or nationalistic, and does not extend to the Russian people.

¶ A papal statement on economic justice went to the president of *Semaines Sociales*, an annual gathering of socially conscious French Catholics. As usual, the Pope steered a middle course between the advocates (if there are any) of completely unregulated capitalism and those of state socialism. Social justice can be realized, he wrote, neither by "the free play of blind economic forces" nor by "an oppressive, omnipotent weighing down on the legitimate autonomy of private initiative."

¶ The Holy Office condemned "corrupt and errant forms of sacred art." Warned the Holy Office: "Of no moment are the objections raised by some that sacred art must be adapted to the necessities and conditions of the present times. For sacred art, which originated with Christian society, possesses its own ends, from which it can never diverge." Although the statement also deplored stereotyped religious art, Vatican spokesmen admitted that it was aimed principally at modern artists who find church decoration a new and challenging technical medium. Wrote Archbishop Celso Costantini: "We are at present in a Babel of art . . . The clamor caused by Matisse decorating the chapel of Vence has not yet died down . . . Chagall would like to paint a Catholic chapel . . . and Picasso has been toying with the idea of decorating a Communist chapel* . . . It is high time to unmask the pretenses of this false art which simply consists of rejecting the human and denying the divine."

Guru's Exit

Paramhansa Yogananda, by his own claim, was the last in a line of four Indian gurus who were "directly commanded" by God to teach the world "the secret yogic

---

RELIGION

science of self-liberation." He moved to the U.S. in 1920 to fulfill his charge. In Southern California he established the headquarters of a Self-Realization Fellowship, with a membership of some 150,000. For more than 30 years he taught his disciples the yoga doctrine that human beings can achieve "god-realization" through their own efforts at disciplining mind and body. Even skeptics testified to his own discipline, *e.g.*, he could slow or speed the pulse in his right wrist, while retaining a normal pulse beat in the left.

For the last two years the guru suffered from a "metaphysically induced illness," as his disciples put it—the result of

© 1952, Self-Realization Fellowship
PARAMHANSA RISING TO MAKE HIS LAST SPEECH*
Devoid of impurities?

"working out" on his own body some of the physical and spiritual burdens of his friends. Last November he began hinting that it was time for him to leave the world. As the weeks passed, the Master grew silent. He finished dictating his spiritual books. His last "little desire" was fulfilled, he said, when a disciple from Florida sent him some green coconut juice in March.

The fellowship's magazine, *Self-Realization*, tells the rest of the story. On March 6, Paramhansa told his disciples laughingly, "I have a big day tomorrow. Wish me luck." The next day he attended a banquet at Los Angeles' Biltmore Hotel for the new Indian ambassador, Binay

---

Ranjan Sen, and his beautiful wife. After eating modestly (vegetables and strawberry parfait), the guru rose to make a speech about "spiritual India." He ended it with a quotation from one of his own poems:

Where Ganges, woods, Himalayan caves, and men dream God—
I am hallowed; my body touched that sod.

As he finished, Paramhansa lifted his eyes, turned slightly to the right and slid to the floor, dead.

Self-Realization disciples claim that their teacher thus performed *mahasamadhi* (a yogi's conscious exit from the body). The medical verdict was "acute coronary occlusion," *i.e.*, a heart attack.

At Forest Lawn Cemetery, where Paramhansa's body was embalmed, officials reported an unusual phenomenon. Wrote Mortuary Director Harry T. Rowe: "No physical disintegration was visible . . . even 20 days after death . . . Paramhansa Yogananda's body was apparently devoid of impurities . . . [His] case is unique in our experience."

Missionary's English

In his 27 years in India and Africa, the Rev. Charles Kingsley* Williams found that English-speaking natives often had trouble understanding the rich prose of the King James Bible. In reading aloud, Missionary Williams came to use his Greek New Testament, translating into simple English as he went along.

When he retired to England 15 years ago, Williams set to work putting his scattered translations together. In London this month, his *New Testament in Plain English* was published, a short, common-sense translation based on an English vocabulary of some 1,500 words. Samples:

¶ *Matthew 6:27:* "And which of you by worrying can add one more hour to his life-time?"

King James version: *"Which of you by taking thought can add one cubit unto his stature?"*

¶ *Luke 6:42:* "You double-dealer, first take the log out of your own eye, and then you will see clearly to take the dust out of your brother's eye."

King James: *"Thou hypocrite, cast out first the beam out of thine own eye, and then shalt thou see clearly to pull out the mote that is in thy brother's eye."*

Methodist Williams intended his New Testament for the mission field, but, said he, "I now find that it can be of use also in this country among those who left school at 16."

---

* Artist Matisse is a vague believer; Marc Chagall is a Jew; Pablo Picasso is a practicing Communist.

* Seated: Mme. Binay Ranjan Sen, wife of the Indian Ambassador, touching her palms in a respectful Hindu greeting (the *pronam*).

* Named for but no kin to famed Charles Kingsley, 19th century clergyman and novelist (*Westward Ho!*), who served as Queen Victoria's chaplain.

TIME, news weekly, presented (on the "Religion" page of its August 4, 1952 issue), the above report of Paramahansa Yogananda's death.

for peace and goodwill among the nations, and referred lovingly to Master as a "spiritual giant." He then announced that Yoganandaji would address the assemblage.

Last Symbolic Tribute

As Paramahansaji rose to go to the speaker's stand, Mme. Sen offered him a gesture of respect by placing her hands together in a *pronam.* It was a true symbolic tribute. By it one feels that the wife of the Ambassador conveyed the gratitude of India to its son in the West who was a living embodiment of its ancient spiritual culture.

(A few minutes later Yoganandaji was no longer a living "embodiment." Happily, Mme. Sen's touching tribute did not go unrecorded. Mr. Say caught in his camera lens the fleeting scene of the *pronam.* The photograph is auspicious not alone for its symbolic value but also because it is the last picture taken of the great guru's living form.*)

Paramahansaji's last speech† appears in full on pages 67-69 inclusive.

Because Master had followed with intense ardor the efforts of Mahatma Gandhi to rescue India from foreign rule without recourse to war, and because the Divine Mother had assured Paramahansaji many years ago that "India will be free in your lifetime," it was naturally a proud night in Master's life when he could publicly welcome to Los Angeles the Ambassador from the new Republic of India. Echoes of that pride in his native land are to be found throughout his brief talk. "I love

---

* About forty minutes after Paramahansaji's passing, a representative of the *Los Angeles Times* arranged to buy from Mr. Say a copy of the *pronam* picture. It appeared in the *Times* on Sunday, March 9, 1952.

† Daya Mata left the anteroom and stood in the Music Room when the speeches started. She recorded stenographically Master's short talk, which was clearly audible over the microphone.

Dr. Rufus B. KleinSmid, chancellor of the University of Southern California, and Mr. Chester Davis, associate director of The Ford Foundation, were to have succeeded Yoganandaji as speakers. Judge Stanley Mosk of the Los Angeles Superior Court was next on the program. Ambassador Sen was supposed to deliver the concluding address of the evening. These scheduled speeches were canceled after Paramahansaji's death.

India," he tells us in a poem, "because there I first learned to love God and all things beautiful."

Yoganandaji's talk was short. (It was over at 9:30 p.m., having lasted less than ten minutes.) He spoke more slowly, more measuredly, than was his wont. The attentive audience was seemingly caught in his magnetic web of love and harmony.

Paramahansaji finished his speech with a few lines from his poem, *My India*. Then, his eyes lifted, he turned slightly to his right and sank quietly to the floor. The great guru's outward mission was ended.

"I was made for Thee alone... My hands were made to serve Thee willingly... My voice was made to sing Thy glory... My feet were made

A sorrowing Ambassador of India gives a brief eulogy of Yoganandaji shortly after his passing. "He was born in India, he lived for India, and he died with the name of India on his lips." The banquet guests stood for several minutes in silence, to honor the great departed soul. Photograph taken at the Biltmore Hotel, Los Angeles, March 7, 1952.

to seek Thy temples everywhere... My eyes were made a chalice to hold Thy burning love... My ears were made to catch the music of Thy footsteps echoing through the halls of space... My lips were made to breathe forth Thy praises."

Those lines written by Master tell of the ideal use of the human body. Now his hands and feet, his eyes and ears and lips — all were stilled. As he departed from that physical form, surely its every atom sang to him in gratitude: *You have used me well.*

Final Rites at SRF Center

Two doctors in the Biltmore Hotel who examined Yoganandaji pronounced him dead. The cause was supposedly a "heart attack" — the name given to any death otherwise inexplicable. On Friday night officers of Forest Lawn Mortuary took Master's sacred body to his third-floor bedroom in the SRF headquarters building. For four days a steady stream of disciples and friends came from far and near, gazing with awe and love on his seraphic face.

The final public rites were held at the Mt. Washington headquarters on Tuesday afternoon, March 11th. A thousand mourners attended.

The ascension ceremony was conducted by Rajarsi Janakananda and Rev. M. W. Lewis. They read inspiring passages from the Bible and the Bhagavad-Gita. Musical selections were played on the pipe organ by Korla Pandit. Shortly after the services had begun, a rainbow of unusually vivid colors appeared in the sky over Mount Washington.

The two-hour services, which ended at 6:00 p.m., were followed by two hours of devotional chanting by Master's disciples. A hundred resident renunciants of his ashrams in southern California filed past the casket, showering the glass lid with rose petals and gazing wih love on the beautiful face of their guru. A serene and spiritually uplifting atmosphere prevailed; all devotees felt Yoganandaji's holy presence among them.

At 10:00 p.m. the casket was removed to Forest Lawn Memorial-Park in the nearby town of Glendale.

Hundreds of floral offerings were received at the headquarters from Master's disciples and friends. Beautiful bouquets and sprays were sent by the numerous SRF Centers in America, Canada, and Mexico. The SRF Center in Honolulu dispatched by airplane a sheaf of anthuriums, *ti* leaves, and rare Hawaiian orchids.

An immense blanket of green ferns, blue irises, and yellow roses, the gift of Rajarsi Janakananda, was placed in front of the casket in the

LAST RITES FOR THE GREAT WORLD TEACHER

The casket with the sacred body of Paramahansa Yogananda as it appeared at the last public rites at Self-Realization Fellowship headquarters. At the conclusion of the service the glass lid of the casket was placed in position by officers of Forest Lawn, and was never again removed.

Yoganandaji's disciples filed past it, chanting *Om Guru* and showering rose petals on the glass lid as a symbol of eternal devotion.

chapel. On the altar, behind the casket, stood a huge arrangement of flowers that depicted the SRF symbol — the white star of the spiritual eye encircled in blue and gold and set within the outline of a lotus flower. The motif of this floral piece, which was sent by the members of the SRF Temple in Hollywood, was carried out in white gladioli, white stocks, blue delphiniums, and yellow daffodils.

Two large floral tributes from Master's disciples at Mount Washington were placed near the head and foot of the casket. One was a circular arrangement of white, blue, and yellow flowers to represent the omniscient spiritual eye; the other was an outline in white stocks of a graceful swan against a background of blue delphiniums.

Lovely flowers were received from many of Paramahansaji's countrymen. The orange, white, and green colors of India's flag were displayed in the floral arrangement sent by Consul General Ahuja and Ambassador Sen. The large green wreath was decorated with orange tulips, orange bird-of-paradise flowers, and white gardenias.

The casket with Paramahansa Yogananda's body is now in a crypt in the "Sanctuary of Golden Slumber" in Holly Terrace of the Great Mausoleum of Forest Lawn Memorial-Park Association in Glendale. His casket will remain there until arrangements can be made for its permanent enshrinement on the spacious grounds of the international headquarters on Mount Washington.

CAPTION FOR PICTURE ON OPPOSITE PAGE

The twin vases with roses at lower right indicate the spot behind which Yoganandaji's casket lies in a crypt at Forest Lawn, Glendale. The statuette near the windows is a small boy in dancing pose, his hands holding cymbals.

When I Am Only a Dream

BY PARAMAHANSA YOGANANDA

I come to tell you all of Him,
And the way to encase Him in your bosom,
And of the discipline that brings His grace.
Those of you who have asked me
To guide you to my Beloved's presence —
I warn you through my silently talking mind,
Or speak to you through a gentle significant glance,
Or whisper to you through my love,
Or loudly dissuade you when you stray away from Him.
But when I shall become only a memory or a mental
      image, or silently speaking voice,
When no earthly call will ever reveal
My whereabouts in unplumbed space,
When no shallow entreaty or stern stentorian command
      will bring from me an answer —
I will smile in your mind when you are right,
And when you are wrong I will weep through my eyes,
Dimly peering at you in the dark,
And weep through your eyes, perchance;
And I will whisper to you through your conscience,
And I will reason with you through your reason,
And I will love all through your love.
When you are able no longer to talk with me,
Read my *Whispers from Eternity;*
Eternally through it I will talk to you.

Unknown I will walk by your side
And guard you with invisible arms.
And as soon as you know my Beloved
And hear His voice in silence,
You will know me again more tangibly than you knew
      me on this earth plane.
And yet when I am only a dream to you
I will come to remind you that you too are naught
But a dream of my Heavenly Beloved,
And when you know you are a dream, as I know now,
We will be ever awake in Him.

Tributes from Ambassador of India, H.E. Binay R. Sen

(From a short talk at Biltmore Hotel, half an hour after Paramahansaji's death on March 7, 1952)

"If we had a man like Paramahansa Yogananda in the United Nations today, probably the world would be a better place than it is. To my knowledge, no one has worked more, has given more of himself, to bind the peoples of India and America together.

"I feel a great personal loss; it is not a personal loss only, but a loss to our country and to this country.

"He was born in India, he lived for India, and he died with the name of India on his lips."

(From a eulogy delivered by Ambassador Sen at Yoganandaji's funeral at SRF headquarters, March 11th)

"I have come here to pay, on my own personal behalf and on behalf of my country, my homage to Paramahansa Yogananda. I met him only a short time ago, but from the moment I first saw him I felt almost overwhelmed by the love he showered on me. I realized that his affection was not so much for me personally as for his country and mine—India.

"Paramahansa Yogananda was a great lover of his country — not in any exclusive sense but for all that India has to offer to the world. He loved mankind as a whole. His philosophy was the philosophy of India.

"After I met him first at this place, Mount Washington Estates, there were several occasions when he came over to meet me. In spite of bodily pain, he made it a point to attend every function that he could.

"I feel it a great honor, a tribute to him, to tell you on this occasion how much you have lost in Paramahansa Yogananda. When we talked we discussed the world situation, the war troubles, and so on. He said that these difficulties will not disappear until man realizes God in man, for in every human being God resides.

"It was this same sense of brotherhood that Christ also preached 2000 years ago. So long as this sense of brotherhood is not accepted and practiced, so long we shall not be able to make anything of this world.

"I feel honored to come here and pay my respects. In a bodily sense Paramahansaji is gone, but in the sense of true brotherhood he has not died.

"Death has no victory in him."

H.E. BINAY R. SEN

ᴋⰅ

The *India News Bulletin,* published by the Embassy of India at Washington, D.C., gives this information:

Binay Ranjan Sen, appointed by the Government of India as the new Ambassador to the U.S.A. in 1951, was born January 1, 1898, and was educated at Calcutta and Oxford Universities. He joined the Indian Civil Service in 1922 and held various administrative and secretariat positions under the Bengal Government, including that of Revenue Secretary. He was Director-General of Food in the Government of India during 1943-45, and was Secretary to the Department of Agriculture 1945-47. In 1947 Mr. Sen was India's Minister at the Washington Embassy, and represented the Government of India on several United Nations agencies.

He led the Indian Delegation to the Economic and Social Council in February 1949 and served again as India's Minister in Washington from March 1949 to March 1950.

He was then posted to Rome as Ambassador and, later, was concurrently accredited as Ambassador to Yugoslavia.

Mr. Sen married Chiroprova Chatterjee in 1931; they have three daughters. The eldest, Nandini, was being educated in the United States at the time Mr. Sen was serving here as Ambassador of India.

Before his retirement in Delhi, Mr. Sen served two terms as Director General of the Food and Agricultural Organization of the United Nations in Rome.

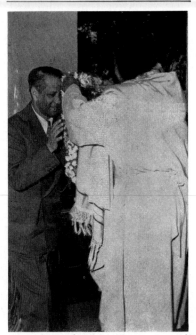

In Indian fashion Paramahansaji welcomes Ambassador Sen to SRF headquarters with a bright garland, March 4, 1952

Last Speech of Paramahansa Yogananda

Delivered at the Biltmore Hotel on March 7, 1952

Your Excellency, our Ambassador, illustrious and understanding Ambassador of free India; Madame Sen; gracious Consul General of India Mr. Ahuja; and Dr. Sharma and Dr. Saund, who have brought such harmony and understanding among the people of India, Pakistan, and America; and all honored guests present here from all nations, all guests present here from my India, my America, and my world: I bow to the God in you.

I am not here in an advisory capacity. So I will relate a few snatches of my experiences. I remember my meeting with Mahatma Gandhi. The great prophet brought a practical method for peace to the warring modern world. Gandhi, who for the first time applied Christ principles to politics and who won freedom for India, gave an example that should be followed by all nations to solve their troubles.

You, your Excellency, represent the great spiritual India. I wish that you bring the very best of my India to my America, and take the very best of my America to my India. But that is a very difficult task, no doubt, for in this world nations and men are all a little bit crazy, and they don't know it — because people with the same kind of craziness mix together. But when differently crazy people get together and compare notes, they find out their particular craziness.

Indeed your Excellency can discover the goodness of different nations. I think if we would gather together the great men of all lands — the great industrialists of America and the good men of all countries — we could build such a model civilization that all nations would eventually form a United World, with God guiding them through their conscience. (*Applause*)

India has great things to give to you, and America can very greatly help India. But people often concentrate on the faults and not on the good qualities of a nation. I remember that just before I first came to America in 1920, I was warned by Hindu friends never to go in dark alleys, lest my scalp be removed by Red Indians! And whenever I saw a bald-headed man I thought some Indians had been at work! (*Laughter*)

I remember, too, that in 1920 I was riding one day to the seashore in Massachusetts when I noticed some "Hot Dog" signs. In imagination I saw all kinds of dogs going through the meat chopper! And I thought, "My Lord, why did You bring me to the land where people eat dogs?" I asked a man what was inside those mysterious bags and he said, "Pork and beef." I gasped in relief to find that Americans don't eat dogs. (*Laughter*)

One morning I was passing by an empty field next to a store. That evening, as I passed that same way again, I saw a house standing in the field. I inquired of a man if the house had been there in the morning. "No," he replied, "they just put it up."

When I think of such energy, I like to be an American. But when I hear of so many American millionaires who die prematurely after making a business success, then I like to be a Hindu — to sit on the banks of the Ganges and concentrate on the factory of Mind from which spiritual skyscrapers can come, and to think of the great masters of India who are her perennial glory. Somewhere between the two great civilizations of efficient America and spiritual India lies the answer for a model world civilization.

It seems there is always plenty of money for war, which brings in its wake great sufferings. We don't seem to learn from these. If we can raise money for wholesale killings, couldn't we picture the possibility that if all big leaders and all peoples got together, they could collect a vast fund that would banish poverty and ignorance from the face of the globe?

I do hope and pray, your Excellency, that you will always emphasize the airplanes of mercy from one country to another instead of airplanes that carry bombs to destroy. Let us work for peace on earth as never before. We want a congress of scientists, of ambassadors, of religious men who will constantly think how to make this world a better home, a spiritual home with God as our Guide. (*Applause*)

I am proud that I was born in India. I am proud that we have a great Ambassador representing my spiritual India. I am very proud today. I often say:

> Mortal fires may raze all her homes and golden paddy fields;
> Yet to sleep on her ashes and dream immortality,
> O India, I will be there!
> God made the earth, and man made confining countries
> And their fancy-frozen boundaries.
> Where Ganges, woods, Himalayan caves, and men dream God —
> I am hallowed; my body touched that sod.

With these last words, from his poem, "My India," Paramahansaji slid to the floor, a beatific smile on his face. He had often said: "I do not wish to die in bed, but with my boots on, speaking of God and India."

TRIBUTE FROM "NEW AGE INTERPRETER"

New Age Interpreter of Los Angeles devoted a page of its April 1952 issue to a tribute to Paramahansa Yogananda. The article follows:

"It was a dramatic and highlighted moment that concluded the remarkable career of Swami Yogananda.* It came March 7th in the Biltmore Hotel in Los Angeles, as he was on the platform concluding a brief talk on his favorite subject of goodwill and fraternal relations between peoples.

---

*His proper title, since 1935, is Paramahansa Yogananda. In December of that year his guru bestowed on him the higher monastic title of "Paramahansa." (*Publisher's Note*)

"Instantly the large audience rose to its feet and remained standing for a brief period of silent prayer, surrounding the Swami with the love his eloquent words had already evoked from their responsive hearts. Under such beneficent auspices it was that his spirit stepped across the border dividing the field of labor here from the sphere of activity over there.

"Swami Yogananda's work was of wide scope, of extraordinary power, and of rich productivity. On the platform and in the classroom he reached great numbers through his lifelong public ministry. His writings were extensive and his teachings attracted a following numbering millions. Among his best known works are *Whispers from Eternity* and *Autobiography of a Yogi*. The latter, published five years ago, is now in its third edition and has been translated into several languages.* It relates many marvels that the author himself experienced.

"Swami Yogananda was born in India. In 1920 he came to this country as a delegate from India to the International Congress of Religions at Boston, and from then on America became his home. In 1925 he founded the Self-Realization Fellowship Church of All Religions with Western headquarters at Mount Washington, Los Angeles, which has centers scattered in all parts of the world. These centers are of three types: study centers, churches, and colonies. Mount Washington is a colony where dedicated ones take up residence and give their full time to the work. In California there are two other colonies, one in Hollywood and another in Encinitas.

"Swami Yogananda made an outstanding cultural and spiritual contribution in furthering the cause of better understanding between East and West. He combined in a conspicuous degree the spiritual idealism of India with practical activity and ability to command material resources which is the dominant characteristic of the West. The two found in him a blend, enabling him to accomplish a work of amazing proportions in the course of no more than three brief decades. The centers he estab-

---

* The book is now in its 11th American edition. It has been published in French, Italian, Spanish, Dutch, German, Swedish, Danish, Icelandic, Greek, Arabic, Japanese, Bengali, Gujarati, Portuguese, Hindi, and Marathi. (*Publisher's Note*)

Memorial Altar, Yogoda Math, Dakshineswar, India, headquarters
of Yogoda Satsanga Society, founded in 1917 by Sri Yogananda

lished, the great numbers he inspired to nobler living, and the ideals
he planted in the common consciousness of humanity will ever remain
a monument to his notable achievement. May his dynamic spirit find
multiplied scope for service in the realm of larger freedom where he
now functions."

The guests of honor stand behind speakers' table (*upper right*). Paramahansaji and Mrs. Sharma stand near the potted palm. (*Left to right, starting with woman in sari standing close to the American flag in upper center of picture*):

Mrs. Frank Chookolingo; Mr. Frank Chookolingo, president, Students' Association of India, Los Angeles; Dr. Rufus B. von KleinSmid, chancellor, University of Southern California, Los Angeles; Mrs. Vernon H.

DINNER OF THE INDIA ASSOCIATION
HONORING
AMBASSADOR B.R. SEN AND MADAME SEN
ON THEIR FIRST VISIT
TO CALIFORNIA
BILTMORE HOTEL, LOS ANGELES MAR. 7, 1952

MASTER'S LAST SPEECH

Gaston; Mrs. B. S. Sungha; Mr. P. L. Bhandari, first secretary, Government of India Information Service, Washington, D.C.; Mr. M. R. Ahuja, Consul General of India, San Francisco, California; Mrs. Chester Davis; H.E. Binay R. Sen, Ambassador of India, Washington, D.C.; Congressman D. S. Saund, president, India Association of America, Los Angeles; Madame Sen, wife of the Ambassador of India; Paramahansa Yogananda; Mrs. J. N. Sharma; Mr. Chester Davis, associate director, The Ford Foun-

A corner of the chapel at SRF headquarters, showing the pipe organ
and a few of the floral tributes from SRF centers

dation, Pasadena, California; Mrs. Mahesh Chandra; Mr. B. S. Sungha;
Mrs. John Anson Ford; Mr. Vernon H. Gaston, president, Los Angeles
Chapter, American Association for the United Nations; Mrs. Bhagat
Singh Thind, president, The American Wives of India, Los Angeles;
Col. A. R. Steinberg.

Among those seated at various tables are: Judge Stanley Mosk, Los
Angeles Superior Court; Mr. Mogens Skott-Hansen, United Nations;
Professor M. S. Sundaram, first secretary, Department of Education,
Government of India, Washington, D.C.; Mr. John Anson Ford, member,
Los Angeles County Board of Supervisors; Mr. and Mrs. G. J. Watumull,
founder, Watumull Foundation, Los Angeles; Dr. Kanta Gupta, organizer
in San Francisco of Famine Relief for India; Mr. Mahesh Chandra,
treasurer, India Association of America; Mr. Ram Bagai, former president,
Hollywood Foreign Correspondents' Association; Mr. Dick Haymes; and
Mr. Frank J. Mackin, Assistant Attorney General, State of California.

Thoughts at the Last Public Rites

Mr. Carroll W. Parcher, publisher of the Glendale, California, *News-Press,* devoted his editorial column on March 13, 1952, to an account of the last public rites for Paramahansaji, as follows:

"Possibly Rudyard Kipling's often quoted verse: 'Oh, East is East, and West is West, and never the twain shall meet, Till earth and sky stand presently at God's great Judgment Seat,' is as true today as when he wrote *The Ballad of East and West* in 1889. But as you watched and heard the combined Hindu and Christian rites at the funeral of Paramahansa Yogananda, one of India's noted religious leaders and founder of Self-Realization Fellowship, you had the feeling that here, perhaps, in the mingling of two of the world's great religious philosophies, might be found a common ground on which the twain might finally meet, after all. Rajarsi Janakananda, new leader of the Fellowship, expressed the same feeling when he said that the East has much to learn from the West, which, in turn, may give to and learn from the East. Binay R. Sen, India's Ambassador to America, said much the same thing in a different way as he eulogized the Paramahansa and his devoted effort to make clear the ancient philosophies of India to the world.

"Ancient Hindu rites of releasing the soul to God expressed the hopes and the beliefs of men everywhere in a life everlasting. 'By the touch of this fire, this body is purified,' the orange-robed monk chanted, touching a lighted splinter of wood to the body of the guru. 'By the touch of this water, this body is returned to its immortal nature,' he continued, and finally: 'By the touch of this sandalwood paste, this body is returned to God with devotion.'

"It may be, you felt, as you listened to the swelling of the organ notes in the universal language of music as produced by the talented fingers of Korla Pandit, and as you watched Hindus and Christians, Indians and Americans, joining together in tribute to a beloved holy man, that in the centuries to come men of different faiths can find unity in a common goal — that the East and the West may finally and happily meet."

MASTER'S BELOVED DISCIPLE RAJARSI CONDUCTS FINAL RITES

Rajarsi Janakananda (*at left, near pillar*) officiated at the funeral of Paramahansa Yogananda, held in the chapel of SRF headquarters, Los Angeles, March 11, 1952. Behind Rajarsi are Yogacharya J. Oliver Black (*left*), leader of Detroit, Michigan, Center; and the late Rev. M. W. Lewis, SRF vice-president. Ambassador Sen, Police Commissioner Somerville (*back to camera*), and Consul General Ahuja are standing directly in front of casket.

Life and Work
of
Paramahansa Yogananda

"An institution is the lengthened shadow of one man." — Emerson

The ideal of love for God and service to humanity found full expression in the life of Paramahansa Yogananda. He came on earth for the purpose of spiritually uniting East and West, to awaken divine yearnings in all hearts. He was practical in his methods; his teachings and life bespoke the wisdom of a true man of God. He carried the maxim of "a sound mind in a sound body" a step further; emphasizing, for the attainment of lasting happiness, the necessity for conscious soul communion with the Infinite Spirit.

Paramahansaji* was born on January 5, 1893, in Gorakhpur, India, near the Himalayas. His father was Sri Bhagabati C. Ghosh, a wealthy executive of the Bengal-Nagpur Railway. Yoganandaji attended Scottish Church College in Calcutta, and Serampore College — an affiliate of Calcutta University, from which, in 1914, he received an A.B. degree. But the mind of the youth was dedicated to a deeper study than that of dry textbooks. From his birth he had but one desire — God-realization.

His search for the Ultimate Goal led him to his guru (spiritual teacher), Swami Sri Yukteswar. In the latter's peaceful Serampore hermitage Paramahansaji received his spiritual training. Sri Yukteswarji was a strict disciplinarian, but the young disciple's devotion never flagged.

---

*The suffix *ji* is a customary respectful addition to names and titles in India; as, Paramahansaji, Yoganandaji, guruji, Gandhiji, etc.

In 1914 Yoganandaji joined the monastic Swami Order.* Sri Yukteswarji told his disciple that, having renounced the ties with a small family of relatives, he must now regard all humanity as his own, to be served as his larger family.

The education of youth was always intensely interesting to Yoganandaji. He established his first school, with seven boys, at Dihika in Bengal in 1917. His work came to the attention of Sir Manindra Chandra Nundy, the Maharaja of Kazimbazar, who in 1918 gave his palace and twenty-five acres in Ranchi as headquarters for the school, which is called

---

* The ancient Swami Order was reorganized in the ninth century by Swami Shankara, India's greatest philosopher. All swamis thus trace their spiritual lineage to the sublime guru Shankara. The Swami Order established by him has retained its prestige to this day under a series of saintly personages — successors in the formal Shankara line.

His Holiness Sri Jagadguru Sri Shankaracharya Bharati Krishna Tirtha of Gowardhan Math, Puri, founded by Shankara, visited America in 1958 under the auspices of Self-Realization Fellowship. During his three-month tour he gave addresses before the leading universities of the country. At a public meeting at Washington and Lee University, His Holiness discussed with Dr. Arnold Toynbee the problems of world peace.

The Swami Order has ten branches. Yoganandaji, like his guru Swami Sri Yukteswarji, belonged to the *Giri* ("mountain") branch.

On joining the Swami Order in 1914, the young yogi was given a monastic name, Yogananda ("bliss through yoga") by his guru. He then relinquished his family names (Mukunda Lal Ghosh), an obligatory procedure for all monks. Yoganandaji was properly addressed as "Swami" until December 1935, at which time his guru bestowed on Yoganandaji a higher spiritual title, that of "Paramahansa."

"Paramahansa" (Supreme Swan) is a title bestowed on a disciple by his guru only after he has attained the unchangeable state of *nirbikalpa samadhi* (irrevocable God-union). The majority of masters in India who have reached the state of a Paramahansa usually remain in seclusion.

Sri Yukteswarji did not bestow the highest of all spiritual titles on his disciple until after Yoganandaji had proved himself by fifteen years of ceaseless work for the spread of yoga in the New World. He then returned to India in August 1935, in answer to his guru's summons, because Sri Yukteswarji was aware that his own time for leaving the earth was drawing near. (Sri Yukteswarji entered *mahasamadhi* on March 9, 1936.)

Yogoda Satsanga Brahmacharya Vidyalaya.* It embodies the educational ideals of India's illumined *rishis* — the sages whose forest ashrams were the ancient seats of learning.

The curriculum includes standard high school subjects as well as yoga concentration, meditation, and the *Yogoda*† system of physical development. The Ranchi institution also maintains an outdoor medical dispensary that offers free surgical and medical aid to many thousands of India's poor. Mahatma Gandhi and many other illustrious personages have visited the unique high school.

In 1920 Yoganandaji began his mission in the West. "Spread to all peoples the knowledge of the self-liberating yoga techniques," his guru Sri Yukteswar had commanded him. Serving as the delegate from India to an International Congress of Religious Liberals, Yoganandaji gave his first speech in America on October 6, 1920, in Boston, Massachusetts.

Audiences Overflowed America's Largest Halls

Paramahansaji then began a series of lectures and classes that eventually took him all over the United States. His teachings were received with unparalleled enthusiasm. Millions of Americans attended his free lectures in the largest available auditoriums in Boston, New York, Buffalo, Rochester, Philadelphia, Pittsburgh, Miami, Washington, Chicago, Detroit, Indianapolis, Cleveland, Cincinnati, Minneapolis, St. Paul, St. Louis, Denver, Salt Lake City, Seattle, Portland, San Francisco, Los Angeles, San Diego, and many other cities. Hundreds of thousands received personal instruction in yoga techniques in the various classes he conducted in America during his ministry of thirty-two years. He also spoke frequently before audiences in churches, societies, clubs, and universities.

He had already begun writing, and in thousands of readers of his books a new spark of adoration for God was kindled by the fervor of Yoganandaji's soul. *The Science of Religion, Metaphysical Meditations,*

---

* The YSS high school in Ranchi, of which Yoganandaji was founder and first Principal, has developed into a complex of schools and colleges. Many alumni of the YSS schools have distinguished themselves in later university life.

† Recharging techniques for health, whose principles of energization were discovered in 1916 by Paramahansa Yogananda.

Cosmic Chants, and *Whispers from Eternity* are books that flowed from his pen like a flood of divine love. Everywhere he found people eager to receive his unifying message — one that shows the true harmony in the scriptures of East and West.

Self-Realization Fellowship (SRF) centers were established in many large cities, and with the help of students Paramahansaji founded in 1925 an international headquarters on Mount Washington Estates in Los Angeles. On the 12-acre estate are ashrams and office buildings for resident monastics who carry on the work of disseminating throughout the world the teachings of Self-Realization Fellowship.

SRF Lessons are Printed at Headquarters

In 1935 the class instructions that Yoganandaji had given on his lecture tours were enlarged and arranged into a series of mimeographed studies, sent out weekly from Los Angeles to SRF members all over the world. In India the same teachings are disseminated from the Yogoda Satsanga Society (YSS) headquarters in Dakshineswar. Both the American and the Indian headquarters possess printing plants, in which *Self-Realization Magazine, Yogoda Magazine,* and other SRF-YSS literature are published.

In 1935 Paramahansaji incorporated his work as a nonsectarian nonprofit institution, Self-Realization Fellowship. To Self-Realization Fellowship he assigned all his possessions in America. Since 1935 the incorporated Fellowship has been enabled to carry on its worldwide work primarily by donations, endowments, and bequests of members and friends.

In June 1935, Yoganandaji left America for eighteen months of travel in England, Scotland, Europe, Palestine, and India.* His yearlong tour of India was a vast triumphal procession. Hundreds of thousands of Indians gathered eagerly to listen to the Master's God-intoxicated speech. He visited the south of India, where for a month he was an official guest of the State of Mysore. He met Sri Ramana Maharshi at

---

* Paramahansaji was widely traveled. He knew India and America from one corner to the other. Previous to his European tour he had visited Ceylon, Japan, Cuba, Mexico, Canada, and Alaska.

Yoganandaji with Lt. Governor (later Governor) of California Goodwin J. Knight, April 8, 1951. The occasion was the dedication of India Center, now called India Hall, a building used for lectures and classes in Self-Realization teachings.

Arunachala, and spent three days in Wardha with Mahatma Gandhi.

Paramahansaji left India in August 1936, and never saw her beloved shores again. Before he departed he made legal arrangements to insure the permanency of the Ranchi school. Two years later a new YSS headquarters was established at a beautiful new ashram in Dakshineswar — "Yogoda Math," on the Ganges River near Calcutta. The spiritual, humanitarian, and educational work he began in his motherland, which work was so dear to his heart, has grown into a nationally known and respected institution.

During 1937 Yoganandaji spent much of his time at a beautiful twenty-three-acre estate in Encinitas, California, now the site of Self-

Realization Fellowship Ashram Center, Encinitas, which includes the Hermitage, where Paramahansaji stayed, a Temple, a Retreat for members, and dormitories for renunciants, including an ashram for postulant monks.

In 1942 an SRF Church of All Religions, designed by Paramahansaji, was built in Hollywood, California. In 1943 another temple was established in San Diego, California. The SRF Church in Long Beach, California, was established in 1947. (In 1968 its congregation was transferred to a larger temple in nearby Fullerton.)

One of Yoganandaji's books, *Autobiography of a Yogi,* published in December 1946, is now a spiritual classic. In its eleventh American edition and ninth London edition, it has been published abroad in many languages.

Founded Two Beautiful Centers in 1950-1951

During the last two years of his life, Paramahansaji founded two more large centers. The twelve-acre SRF Lake Shrine at Pacific Palisades, California, with an inspiring Mahatma Gandhi World Peace Memorial, was opened to the public in August 1950. Eight months later, on April 8, 1951, a spiritual and cultural meeting place, "India Center," in Hollywood, California, was dedicated by Paramahansaji in the presence of Mr. M. R. Ahuja, Consul General of India; Mr. Goodwin J. Knight, Lt. Governor of California, and hundreds of other guests.

Self-Realization Fellowship has many branch centers and meditation groups on four continents. In southern California there are six large centers: the international headquarters in Los Angeles, and ashram centers and temples in Hollywood, Pacific Palisades, Fullerton, Encinitas and San Diego.

The simple young monk who in 1920 had come — with only modest funds, and without a single friend save God — to the New World, accomplished there a herculean work. The priceless training he gave his disciples, the words of comfort and wisdom in his books, and the many hermitages and churches and centers he founded remain as evidence of his all-embracing love for humanity.

Though Paramahansaji often longed to roam in simplicity by the

Paramahansa Yogananda's sitting room at Self-Realization Fellowship international headquarters, Los Angeles, California

Ganges or in the Himalayas, meditating on the Cosmic Beloved, he humbly obeyed his guru's behest to spread in the West the yoga teachings of India. With phenomenal energy and undiscourageable enthusiasm Paramahansa Yogananda successfully assumed the tremendous burden of planning and putting into motion a worldwide organization. Through it he has made the liberating message of Self-realization and Yoga available to all men.

I Shall Be a Messenger of Joy

I desire no monuments in the halls of fame. After death I shall enter countless caves of soul love and secretly inspire my brothers with dulcet spiritual thoughts.

Unknown, I shall be a gentle ghostly messenger of joy. I shall visit the dark mounds in human minds — the graves of bright aspirations. There I shall light hope candles fashioned in my nook of silence.

— Paramahansa Yogananda

Some of the speakers at a Memorial Meeting for Paramahansa Yogananda, April 26, 1952, Ram Mohan Library Hall, Calcutta, India. The life-size oil painting of Paramahansaji is the work of his younger brother, Sananda Lal Ghosh, distinguished Bengali artist.

A huge gathering was present to honor the *mahasamadhi* of the beloved Master. Conveners of the meeting included Nirmal Chandra Chundur, Mayor of Calcutta, and many eminent judges, educators, religious leaders, editors, and statesmen. Speakers shown on the dais are: C. C. Biswas, Judge, Calcutta High Court, and Law Minister, Government of India; Charu Chandra Ganguly, former Chief Judge, Calcutta S.C. Court; Nripendra Nath Bose, advocate; B. Chowdhury, barrister-at-law; Swami Atmananda Giri, secretary, YSS; Dr. N. N. Das, professor, Calcutta University, and dear boyhood friend of Paramahansaji, who visited Master in Los Angeles in 1950; Dr. Saroj Kumar Das, professor, Calcutta University; Manick Lal De, famous devotional singer; Fanindra Mohan Dutt of the Imperial Bank of India; Prabhas Chandra Ghosh, beloved cousin of Paramahansaji, and vice-president of YSS; Indra Nath Seth, Calcutta pleader, and translator of *Autobiography of a Yogi* into Bengali; Sanat Kumar Chatterjee, Calcutta merchant; Bejoy Krishna Mullick, noted devotional singer; Sananda Lal Ghosh and Bishnu Charan Ghosh, brothers of Paramahansaji; Bhibhusan Bhattacharya, student at Yogoda Math; Krishna M. Majumdar, engineer; and Haradhon Ghosh, Yogoda Math.

Memorial Services in India

For three years Yoganandaji planned to visit India. But in talks about the trip he always added "if Divine Mother wills it." His secretary made reservations on the *Queen Mary,* for Paramahansaji and a small party, first for 1950 (October 11), then for 1951 (October 23), and finally for 1952 (August 27). All passports had been ready for a long time. Master would not give a definite reply to questions from disciples about the matter. "We will see what the Lord has in store for me," he would say in his sweet, humble way.

Services at Yogoda Math, YSS Headquarters in India

Yogoda Math, YSS-SRF headquarters in Dakshineswar, Bengal, India, sent Self-Realization Fellowship the following report:

March 9, 1952, was for us an ominous day. When, at 10 a.m., we received Rajarsi Janakananda's cable—a bolt from the blue!—we were engulfed in abysmal depths of grief. For us it was life's darkest hour. The news left us stunned; our senses were numbed with an inexplicable feeling. We had been getting ready for the Sunday services; upon receiving the news we immediately put off our shoes (in India a mark of respect) and met in the prayer hall to pay homage to the great departed soul of Paramahansaji and to observe the day with fasting and prayers.

Upon receipt of another cable the following day, advising us of the date and time of the services to be held in Los Angeles, the disciples, friends, relatives, and admirers of Paramahansaji were duly informed, and they individually and congregationally observed those hours by silent prayers and meditations.

According to Hindu custom, a mourning period of ten days was observed, during which time Paramahansaji's disciples walked barefooted, took oil-less baths, refrained from shaving, and strictly followed the vegetarian diet enjoined for a *brahmachari* (one who practices self-con-

trol). At the end of the mourning period the disciples shaved their
beards, trimmed hair and nails, and then bathed in the holy waters of
the Ganges in front of Yogoda Math. They gathered in the prayer room
at the Guru Mandir ("Hall of the Gurus") of Yogoda Math. It was
beautifully decorated with circles of lilies and other pure-white flowers
fashioned into crosses and garlands, many of which were arranged over
large portraits of Paramahansaji in different poses. The pictures were
placed on a dais decorated with the Yogoda lotus emblem, executed
in copper, that was constructed so as to diffuse from its core a subdued
golden light.

A special service was conducted by Swami Atmananda, with *puja*
(worship, homage) for the beloved Gurudeva, and offerings of his
favorite dishes. Selected passages from Paramahansaji's writings and
from the Bengali *Ananteyr Dhaney* (*Whispers from Eternity*) were read
by Sri Prabhas Chandra Ghosh and Sri Indra Nath Seth. As is customary

on such occasions, a *kirtan* (song), melodious and soul-inspiring, was sung by Sri Bijoy Krishna Mullick. The spellbound audience felt the vibrations and all-pervading presence of the sublime soul of Paramahansaji.

On March 23rd a *bhandara** was held in memory of the blessed master Yoganandaji. On this occasion a large *shamiana* (canopy) was erected on the spacious lawn of Yogoda Math. Decorations of white lilies, floral circles, crosses, garlands, and wreaths were everywhere in evidence, and pictures of the four great gurus of YSS-SRF (Mahavatar Babaji, Lahiri Mahasaya, Sri Yukteswarji, and Paramahansa Yoganandaji) were placed on the poles of the *pandal* (temporary pavilion).

The *brahmacharis* of Yogoda Math read the scriptures of *Bhagavad-Gita* and *Chandi* throughout the whole day. *Sannyasis* (renunciants) of various sects and religions, as well as friends, relatives, and disciples of Paramahansaji came from all parts of Bengal to do him honor.

An *Om* song (chant describing the spiritual bliss felt by the devotee when he listens within to the Cosmic Symphony of *Om,* the *Amen,* or Holy Ghost Vibration), was sung by the golden-voiced Sri Nirmal Kumar Baral. Sri Jananendra Nath Mukherji, revered disciple of the great master Swami Pranabananda ("the saint with two bodies"), presided over the meeting and addressed the assemblage.

"The great soul that is Paramahansaji came on earth with a tremendous mission," Sri Jananendra said. "You need not be overwhelmed with grief for his passing away from this world. Freed from the limitations of flesh and blood he has entered into Eternity, and his all-pervading spirit will now act more widely through all of you.

"To pay respect to him truly is to follow his teachings, sincerely to practice *Kriya Yoga,* and to spread the timeless message of the great gurus of India."

A group of five hundred persons was present and followed the ceremony with deep reverence and devotional fervor.

---

*A ceremonial feast given in honor of a departed great soul. Readers of *Autobiography of a Yogi* will remember Master's account (chapter 42) of the *bhandara* feast he arranged on March 21, 1936, to honor the memory of his own guru, Swami Sri Yukteswarji. (*Publisher's Note*)

Playing of a Record of Master's Voice *

Paramahansaji's voice was heard when the recording of his song, "O God Beautiful," was played, and the entire audience felt a thrill of inspiration sweep over them as they listened to his voice. A calm and serene atmosphere pervaded the ceremony, leaving an indelible impression on all that Paramahansaji's sweet eternal spirit hovered near, shedding the effulgence of his immortal blessings, and giving them courage and bright hopes for the future. Each one felt a new enthusiasm to carry on Yoganandaji's sacred mission on earth, to spread the immortal message of the great gurus, and to share with the world the religious, moral, and cultural heritage of India.

A touching song by Sri Manick Lal Dey concluded the ceremony. The guests then shared a sumptuous repast. As is customary in India after a *bhandara* charitable gifts and food were distributed among the poor.

Ten-Day Mourning Period Observed in Ranchi, India

Yogoda Satsanga Brahmacharya Vidyalaya, boys' school founded by Paramahansa Yogananda in 1918 in Ranchi, was closed for seven days, from March 10th through March 16th, to observe mourning for the passing of the great guru. The students of the *Vidyalaya* observed a day of fasting, with prayers and songs in honor of the revered Master.

The disciples of Paramahansaji, and other devotees and members of the *Yogoda Satsanga* Ashram in Ranchi, observed a ten-day mourning period, following the strict disciplines and rituals enjoined by the Hindu scriptures.

On March 18th a memorial service was held. The prayer hall was decorated with flowers and green leaves; a large picture of Master was beautifully garlanded, and sweet-smelling flowers were heaped on the raised platform. Incense, symbolizing purity, was burned, and special prayers were offered, with chanting of ancient Sanskrit scriptures and devotional songs. *Hom-yajna* (burning of sacrificial fire) was then performed, and Vedic *mantras* (chants) were intoned. The *Bhagavad-*

---

*Yoganandaji made phonograph recordings of several Hindu chants.

Gita in its entirety was read aloud, followed by *kirtan* (the singing of loving songs to God).

At noon *sannyasis* (renunciants), mendicants, and beggars (*daridranarayan*) were fed. *Proshad* (food offered to God) was distributed among 200 YSS devotees. In the afternoon several chapters from Paramahansaji's *Autobiography of a Yogi* were read to the assemblage.

On the following day, March 19th, another large gathering was held at the *Vidyalaya*, at which time the events of Paramahansaji's holy life were reviewed.

Taking part in this function were: Lt. Col. A. K. Ghosh, Chief Medical Officer, YSS *Sevashram* (Home of Service); Probodh Chandra Mukherjee, Officer, Forest Dept., Government of Bihar; Sasanka Shakher Chakraverty, Zamindar; B. N. Sayaya, *Munsiff* (Judge), Ranchi; Mr. Amar Nath Jahar, Chief Electrical Engineer, Ranchi; Mr. A. B. Saran, Superintendent, Ranchi Technical School; Sj. Bishnu Dutt Bhargav, Chief Engineer, R. K. Budhia & Sons; Prof. Manash Ranjan Banerjee, St. Xavier's

Part of the gathering at Memorial Service for Yoganandaji, Yogoda Math, India. An outdoor pavilion was erected for the occasion.

College, Ranchi; F. N. Aikat and H. L. Mukherjee, government contractors; and Mr. Dinanath Singh, Municipal Commissioner, Ranchi.

Distinguished Men of Bengal Convene a Meeting

A group of prominent men of Bengal convened a memorial meeting, in honor of Yoganandaji's *mahasamadhi*, on April 26th at Ram Mohan Library Hall in Calcutta. The distinguished conveners of the meeting issued a printed invitation card. Their names follow:

The Most Reverend Arabindo Nath Mukerjee, Anglican Church, Lord Bishop of India, Pakistan, Burma, and Ceylon; Hon. Mr. Justice S. N. Bannerjee; Hon. Mr. Justice Rupendra Coomar Mitra; Hon. Mr. Justice Ramaprosad Mukherjee; Dr. Anil Krishna De; Sri Jagabandhu Bose; Tarun Kanti Ghose, member, Bengal Legislative Assembly; Panna Lal Bose, member, Bengal Legislative Assembly; Dr. Shyama Prasad Mookerjee, a leader of Hindu Mahasabha, one of the six major political parties of India; Jnananjan Niyogi, active in the political life of the nation; Charu Chandra Ganguli, Chief Judge (retired); Nirmal Chundur Chundur, solicitor; Bibhuti Roy Chowdhuri, bar-at-law; Tushar Kanti Ghose, editor, *Amrita Bazar Patrika;* Suresh Chandra Majumdar, editor, *Hindusthan Standard* and *Ananda Bazar Patrika;* Vivekananda Mukherji, editor, *Jugantar;* Bhabatosh Roy, editor, *Hindu;* K. C. Agarwala, editor, *Advance* and *Viswamitra;* Rabindra Nath Gupta, Indian Police Service (retired); Nandadulal Sreemany, Debendra Nath Mukherjee, Damodardas Khannah, and Dr. Saroj Kumar Das.

The speeches at the meeting, which were reported in the large Calcutta dailies, lauded Paramahansaji as the ideal teacher of East and West. The gathering was presided over by The Honorable Mr. C. C. Biswas, Bengal Minister of State for External Affairs.

"Groveling, man knows well; despair is seldom alien; yet these are perversities, no part of man's true lot. The day he wills, he is set on the path to freedom. Too long has he hearkened to the dank pessimism of his "dust-thou-art" counselors, heedless of the unconquerable soul."

— *Paramahansa Yogananda*

TO GURUJI

By Grace Thompson Seton

A saint has trod our paths, smiled
on these hills,

Planted these roses in the desert
sands,

Interpreted for us these sacred
books

And for us built these walls of
stone and mortar —

Man's temples for worship of the
Father.

Dear Swan of Heaven,* you made
us know

Love and charity, goodness
incarnate.

No longer can we wear the old
drab cape

Of ignorance and selfishness
and grief.

Now we must weave a shimmer-
ing girdle

Of God-born thoughts you ever
sought to spread

Among the thousands of your
straying ones

Plodding the human path of
Calvary.

Bless us with your ever guiding
love,

* *Paramahansa,* "Supreme Swan"

The perfume of your teaching.
Attar, pure, flowing
From the Infinite...
This we may treasure
In the full chalice
Of rememberings.

Lift high our vision.
We who touched the hem
Of your robe of godly life
Shall not forget.

A colored photograph of Yoganan-
daji is garlanded with love at the
Memorial Service held in Yogoda
Math, Dakshineswar, India.

The body of the blessed master, Paramahansa Yogananda, as it lay on his bed three days after his passing. The "phenomenal state of immutability" that manifested itself at his death appears to be God's dramatic way of calling mankind's attention to the soul-revealing science of yoga.

Why Does a Great Master Suffer?

The last two years of Paramahansaji's life, so filled with activities — the founding of SRF Lake Shrine and Gandhi Memorial in Pacific Palisades and of India Center in Hollywood, the completion of many writings, the supervision of a thousand organizational duties that fall on the shoulders of a leader of a worldwide movement — were yet years of physical illness.

Why should a great master suffer? This point was considered by Yoganandaji in his *Autobiography of a Yogi* (chapter 21), in which he told of his own guru Sri Yukteswarji's sickness in Kashmir. The explanation follows:

"The metaphysical method of physical transfer of disease is known to highly advanced yogis. A strong man may assist a weak one by helping the latter to carry a heavy load; a spiritual superman is able to minimize the physical and mental troubles of his disciples by assuming a part of their karmic burdens. Just as a rich man relinquishes some money when he pays off a large debt for his prodigal son, who is thus saved from the dire consequences of his folly, so a master willingly sacrifices a portion of his bodily wealth to lighten the misery of disciples. *

"By a secret yogic method, the saint unites his mind and astral vehicle with those of a suffering individual; the disease is conveyed, wholly or in part, to the yogi's fleshly form. Having harvested God on the physical field, a master is no longer concerned with his body. Though he may allow it to become diseased in order to relieve other persons, his mind, unpollutable, is not affected. He considers himself fortunate in being able to render such aid. To achieve final salvation in the Lord is indeed to find that the human body has completely fulfilled its purpose; a master then uses it in any way he deems fit.

---

* Many Christian saints, including Therese Neumann, are familiar with the metaphysical transfer of disease.

"A guru's work in the world is to alleviate the sorrows of mankind, whether through spiritual means or intellectual counsel or will power or physical transfer of disease. Escaping to the superconsciousness whenever he so desires, a master can become oblivious of physical illness; sometimes, to set an example for disciples, he chooses to bear bodily pain stoically. By putting on the ailments of others, a yogi can satisfy, for them, the karmic law of cause and effect. This law is mechanically or mathematically operative; its workings may be scientifically manipulated by men of divine wisdom.

"The spiritual law does not require a master to become ill whenever he heals another person. Healings ordinarily take place through the saint's knowledge of various methods of instantaneous cure in which no hurt to the spiritual healer is involved. On rare occasions, however, a master who wishes to quicken greatly his disciples' evolution may then voluntarily work out on his own body a large measure of their undesirable karma.

"Jesus signified himself as a ransom for the sins of many. With his divine powers,* Christ could never have been subjected to death by crucifixion if he had not willingly cooperated with the subtle cosmic law of cause and effect. He thus took on himself the consequences of others' karma, especially that of his disciples. In this manner they were highly purified and made fit to receive the omnipresent consciousness or Holy Ghost that later descended upon them.†

"Only a Self-realized master can transfer his life force or convey into his own body the diseases of others. An ordinary man cannot employ this yogic method of cure; nor is it desirable that he should do so, because an unsound physical instrument is a hindrance to deep meditation. The Hindu scriptures teach that an imperative duty of man is to keep his body in good condition; otherwise his mind is unable to remain fixed in devotional concentration.

"A very strong mind, however, can transcend all physical difficulties

---

* Christ said, just before he was led away to be crucified: "Thinkest thou that I cannot now pray to my Father, and he shall presently give me more than twelve legions of angels? But how then shall the scriptures be fulfilled, that thus it must be?" — *Matt.* 26:53-4.   † *Acts* 1:8 and 2:1-4.

and attain to God-realization. Many saints have ignored illness and succeeded in their divine quest. St. Francis of Assisi, himself severely afflicted with ailments, healed other men, and even raised the dead....

"Many persons believe that a great master should have the health and strength of a Sandow.* The assumption is unfounded. A sickly body does not indicate that a guru is lacking in divine powers, any more than lifelong health necessarily indicates inner illumination. The distinguishing qualifications of a master are not physical but spiritual.

"Numerous bewildered seekers in the West erroneously think that an eloquent speaker or writer on metaphysics must be a master. Proof that one is a master, however, is supplied only by the ability to enter at will the breathless state (*sabikalpa samadhi*) and by the attainment of immutable bliss (*nirbikalpa samadhi*).† The *rishis* have pointed out that solely by these achievements may a human being demonstrate that he has mastered *maya*, the dualistic cosmic delusion. He alone may say from the depths of realization: *'Ekam sat'* ('Only One exists')."

Who Would Wish "Immortal Life" Physically?

"Verily, verily, I say unto you, if a man keep my saying [remain unbrokenly in the Christ Consciousness], he shall never see death" — (*John* 8:51). Paramahansaji explained this saying in *Autobiography of a Yogi*, as follows:

"In these words Jesus was not referring to immortal life in the physical body — a monotonous confinement one would hardly mete out to a sinner, much less a saint! The illumined man of whom Christ spoke is one who has awakened from the deathly trance of ignorance to Eternal Life.

"Man's essential nature is formless omnipresent Spirit. Compulsory

---

* A German athlete (d. 1925), known as "the world's strongest man."

† In *sabikalpa samadhi* the devotee has spiritually progressed to a state of inward divine union, but cannot maintain his cosmic consciousness except in the immobile trance-state. By continuous meditation, he reaches the superior state of *nirbikalpa samadhi*, where he moves freely in the world and performs his outward duties without any loss of God-realization.

or karmic embodiment is the result of *avidya,* ignorance. The Hindu scriptures teach that birth and death are manifestations of *maya,* cosmic delusion. Birth and death have meaning only in the world of relativity.

"Great masters like Pranabananda* who come back to earth in new embodiments do so for reasons best known to themselves. Their incarnations on this planet are not subject to the rigid restrictions of karma. Such voluntary returns are called *vyutthana* or reversion to earthly life after *maya* has ceased to blind.

"Whatever be the manner of his passing, whether ordinary or phenomenal, a fully God-realized master is able to resurrect his body and to appear in it before the eyes of earth dwellers. Materializing the atoms of a physical body can scarcely strain the powers of one who is united with the Lord — Him whose solar systems defy computation!"

"I lay down my life that I might take it again," Christ proclaimed. "No man taketh it from me, but I lay it down of myself. I have power to lay it down, and I have power to take it again" (*John* 10:17-18).

---

* Chapter 3 of *Autobiography of a Yogi* tells of Yoganandaji's meeting with Swami Pranabananda, "the saint with two bodies," an exalted disciple of Lahiri Mahasaya; in chapter 20 an account is given of Pranabanandaji's passing and his swift return to earth in a new body in which he joined the sacred group around Mahavatar Babaji in the Himalayas.

CAPTION FOR PICTURE ON OPPOSITE PAGE   →

H.E. Binay R. Sen, Ambassador of India; Hon. M. R. Ahuja, Consul General of India; and Dr. John A. Somerville, Los Angeles Police Commissioner, stand by Yoganandaji's bier before the chapel altar at Self-Realization Fellowship / Yogoda Satsanga Society of India international headquarters, Los Angeles, at the last public rites, March 11, 1952.

In his eulogy of Paramahansaji on this occasion, the Ambassador said: "Death found no victory in him." Later events proved that His Excellency's words were literally true. After death Yoganandaji's body did not manifest the usual signs of dissolution.

Paramahansa Yogananda:

An Appreciation

By **MULK RAJ AHUJA**
Consul General of India

Consulate of India
San Francisco, California
March 28, 1952

When I first called on Yoganandaji about a year and a half ago it was more out of curiosity than any other consideration. Since my appointment a few months earlier I had heard many conflicting reports about him and his work and I must confess that when I met him my mind was not entirely devoid of suspicion. I was, however, hardly a few minutes with him before the impact of the greatness of his soul and the sincerity of his purpose began to dispel the doubts that had clouded my mind. Before the visit ended my heart began to glow with the warmth and love that he radiated.

When I stepped out of Mount Washington I knew that I was taking with me more than mere goodwill or kinship. After our first meeting the attraction we felt for each other did not have to wait long for us to be tied together in bonds of love and affection which even death cannot cut asunder.

Apart from the charm and beauty of his physical being, which was no doubt the index of the soul he possessed, Paramahansaji's deep affection and love for humanity — including even those unfriendly and reluctant to share in his faith — gave him a stature among his fellow beings which it would be difficult to match.

He brought to America from the country of his birth the serenity of soul and the understanding of the human and spiritual values of life which not only helped many a man high and low to obtain peace of mind in modern society but also helped in an understanding between the peoples of India and the U.S.A.

As an apostle of peace and a believer in the brotherhood of man, Yoganandaji devoted his life and all the energy and means he possessed to the cause of understanding and friendship between the East and the West. To him India and the U.S.A. were not two separate countries but the two component parts of one single plan for the development in harmony of both material and spiritual values of man.

As his thoughts and actions throughout his life, so his last words "My America—My India" represented his mission on earth.

Yogananda cannot and shall not die; for his immortal soul will ever beckon, guide, and inspire his millions of followers and admirers on to the path leading to the brotherhood of man.

Paramahansa Yogananda: *In Memoriam*

By **SAROJ KUMAR DAS**, Ph.D.

Professor, University of Calcutta, India

While gazing at the photographic reproductions in *Self-Realization Magazine* of the lying-in-state of Paramahansa Yogananda, and while reading the accounts of his last activities and talks, and, above all, the thrilling testimony of Mr. Harry T. Rowe, Mortuary Director of Forest Lawn Memorial-Park in California, I confess to have been overwhelmed by the compelling majesty of the ascended soul, coupled with the epic grandeur of his journey's end. My impression of the scene is one of ineffable mystery and transcendent beauty, defying expression in words. That emotional reaction, as remembered in tranquillity, lends itself to an instructive comparison with an invocative hymn of Tagore's, one that was designed in worshipful adoration of another World Teacher: "O thou Life all-embracing! O thou Death all-enlightening!" (*Hey mahajivana, hey mahamarana*).

The report in *Self-Realization Magazine* tells us that on the afternoon of the day preceding that of his ascension "the Master sang over and over the ancient Bengali chant for which Tagore wrote the words: *In my house with Thine own hands light the lamp of Thy love... Change my darkness to Thy light, change my darkness to Thy light*"—which in the original read thus: "*Amara ey gharey apanara karey griha deepakhani jwalo... parasmanir pradeepa tomara, achapala tar jyoti sona korey labey palakey amara sakala kalanka kalo.*"

Paramahansaji's last act of ministration through this favorite song of his was at once prophetic and symbolic — dissolving itself in a crescendo reminiscent of that typical prayer by the apostle of Light which has since become famous: "Not more life, O God, but more light!" Nearly three thousand years ago did Buddha, the Enlightened, exhort his disciples, in the manner of the Master and Founder of Self-Realization Fellowship, to a life of self-illuminating inspiration in words of undying memory, *"Attodipo bhava,"* that is, "Be a shining lamp unto others."

In the manner of the Master's passing — specifically the prelude to and preparation for it — death appears as the last fulfillment of a life of self-dedication. In such an inspiring context one remembers Maeterlinck's sentiment: "Without death what would life be? It is death that gives life its weight, its importance, its dignity, its meaning, and its infinite perspectives."

Verily, it is Death that gives Life its infinite perspectives. One such perspective in the present case is the extraordinary revelation, in the words of the Mortuary Director, of "the absence of any visual signs of decay in the dead body of Paramahansa Yogananda. Had the muscle protein and blood stream of the deceased not been comparatively free of bacteria, deterioration of the body could have set in as early as six hours after life had departed. No physical disintegration was visible in Paramahansa Yogananda's body even twenty days after death." For these reasons the mortician asserts that "the case of Paramahansa Yogananda is unique in our experience."

This is as it should be. Paramahansa, flawlessly perfect soul that he was, could not possibly have chosen for tenement a body that was not in pre-established harmony with the purest conceivable soul. In point of fact the Master, as a liberated soul, was *in* the world but not *of* it. Very much like the chariot of the hero Yudisthira, that would ever keep several inches above the ground in its drive on the battlefield of Kurukshetra and thus escape contact with dirt and impurities, so did Yoganandaji live up consistently to the ideal of a perfected soul and thereby justify his title of Paramahansa ("supreme swan"). If man, as Schopenhauer has taught us, is the union of the soul and the body, the body being the objectification of the will, which is the essence of the soul, here at least we have a typical case.

The last though not the least important feature of Paramahansa Yogananda's missionary career is an unprecedented and unique dimension of values, imparted to the Self-Realization Fellowship mission itself. Many adventures of ideas in this line have miscarried — by stopping, as things of arrested development, at a convenient limit, and thus failing to reach the Promised Land.

Three centuries ago the Pilgrim Fathers started to colonize the New World. In 1920 Yogananda, all unfriended and unchartered, first set foot on America with a divinely appointed mission of Self-Realization Fellowship to uplift humanity. The unflagging romance of that "flight of the alone to the Alone" has got to be told to generations yet unborn. What now behooves us to do is to meditate on and marvel at the fructifying power of that seminal idea of Self-Realization Fellowship, which, within three decades, has radiated its influence in America and elsewhere in the shape of numerous Fellowship Centers.

Emulating the "cult of the Wayfarer," Paramahansa Yogananda pursued with vertical consistency "the morality of the Open Road" right into the heart of the Promised Land. In other words, he lived his way into Reality; and that accounts for his compelling greatness and supremacy.

Harnack, celebrated authority of Christological scholarship, said: "Christ could think of no better task than to point men to Himself." With no loss of meaning can the words be said of Paramahansa Yogananda! It recalls a remote parallel of this spiritual truth, in and through

─────────────────────────────

CAPTION FOR PICTURE ON OPPOSITE PAGE   →

The body of the blessed master as it appeared at the final public rites on March 11, 1952. The flags of America and India stand amidst a wealth of flowers. The green wreath of white gardenias and orange tulips (*shown near the top of the casket*) displays the three colors of India's flag. It was sent by Ambassador Sen and Consul General Ahuja.

the ceaseless march of Prince Rohita in the *Aitareya Brahmana* of the
Rig-Veda:

*Charam vai madhu vindati Charan Swadum udumvaram Pashya Sury-
yasya Shremanam Yo na tandrayate charan Charaiveti, Charaiveti.*

(Verily, by moving forward, man enjoys the elixir of life, the life
everlasting. Look at the sun, which, in its ceaseless movement, is never
caught napping. Move forward, therefore, move on and on!) Does
the thought not find an exact echo in Walt Whitman's *Song of the Open
Road,* voicing the soul of the coming new world-order:

"Allons! Whoever you are, come travel with me!
Traveling with me you find what never tires....
Be not discouraged, keep on, there are divine things well envelop'd."

When all is said and done, the momentous fact that stands out
against the background of Paramahansa's ascension is his utterance,
with a redemptive grace for erring mankind, before the high altar of
the Divine Mother, invoked for that act of last ministration:

"My India! My America!"

Who else except a realized Self could have thus encompassed the
land of his birth and the land of his adoption in the capacious com-
prehension of an ever-expansive love, and sent an emotional thrill as
much as a spiritual appeal through countless minds of both these lands?
And it was an utterance, be it remembered, that was authenticated by
the presence of the official representative* of the Indian Republic.

Generations hereafter will cherish this epochal occasion as a land-
mark, indicating the rediscovery of the soul of America, helping to pave
the way toward that "One World" which is yet to be.

When comes such another Master and World Teacher?

---

*Ambassador Binay R. Sen.

Yoga and the Miracle of Incorruption

*Weeks after his death, the unchanged face of Paramahansa Yogananda
shone with the divine luster of incorruptibility.*

By Paramahansa Yogananda's perfect and selfless life, and by his
death and its phenomenal sequel, the Heavenly Father has given the
world an example of the value of yoga. This devotee of God was indeed
well named Yogananda — "divine bliss through yoga." The yogic techniques for God-realization anciently developed by India's sages constitute
the highest science known to man.

Other devotees of God, Christian saints who manifested bodily
immutability not through yoga but through extraordinary powers of
singlehearted aspiration toward the Divine, were St. John of the Cross
and St. Teresa of Avila. The body of St. John, who died in 1591, was
exhumed in 1859 and found to be in a state of incorruptibility. The body
of St. Teresa, which lies in a church at Alba in Spain, has for four
centuries remained intransmutable. The site has witnessed innumer-
able miracles.

Paramahansa Yogananda was a world teacher, a universal guru. His
difficult mission on earth was to awaken the nations to the soul-revealing
possibilities of yoga. During his ministry of more than thirty years in
America and abroad, he himself bestowed *Kriya Yoga* initiation on more
than 100,000 students, and gave certain preliminary yoga techniques
to hundreds of thousands of others — those who attended, in one large
American city or another, his yoga classes.

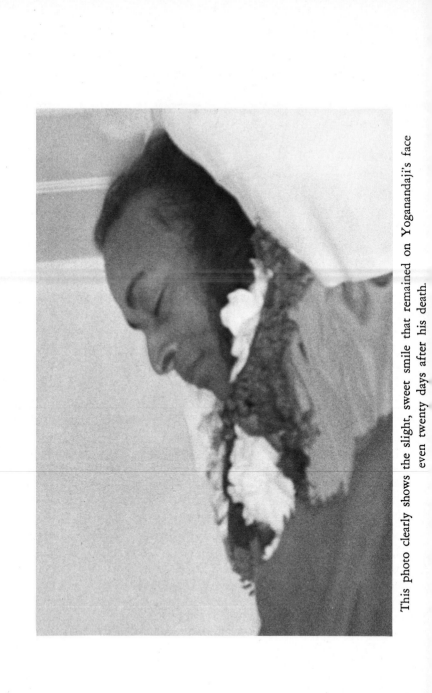

This photo clearly shows the slight, sweet smile that remained on Yoganandaji's face even twenty days after his death.

Yogananda was a fearless spiritual warrior, a pioneer for a new and better age. When he arrived in the West in 1920, few Americans had any knowledge of yoga, whether theoretical or practical. Today vast numbers of Westerners look reverently on the science of yoga because Yogananda came to live among them and to teach them its sublimity.

Besides personally instructing students in yoga, the compassionate guru worked long and devotedly to serve truth seekers in distant cities and countries, those who could not make the necessary journey to meet a great master face to face. How many nights he sat at his desk, writing out a new lesson for a beloved family of SRF members! Whether near or far, they were permitted to receive weekly lessons on the right conduct of life and the well balanced development of man's threefold nature — physical, mental, and spiritual. The simple *Kriya Yoga* instructions, also, are sent to SRF members after they have fulfilled certain requirements, which include a period of study of preliminary teachings.

Master was a tireless teacher. He left no avenue unapproached in his efforts to accomplish his task. Whether training disciples, lecturing, sitting in silent meditation, teaching classes, traveling at home or abroad, attending meetings or social functions, writing books, publishing magazines, sending lessons by mail, granting interviews, founding centers, or living in every respect an ideal life, Paramahansaji had but one humble desire — to please God by serving humanity.

Master's life span embraced a period of two World Wars and the ushering in of a new era, the Atomic Age. A spiritual awakening must take place in the hearts of men, lest they perish ignominiously by misuse of the prodigious atomic energies — energies that the Lord permitted scientists to discover for more useful ends, surely, than wholesale slaughter. A lasting spiritual understanding in the minds of men, by which alone war can be averted, cannot be brought about merely by outward means such as talks, conferences, and so on, but by yoga — "union" in consciousness of man with God, of the creature with his Creator.

To arouse that understanding in the minds of many Americans was a task that only a great yogi could have accomplished. Hindu teachers in this country who had never received training in India under a great master were unable to shed any light for Westerners on the ancient science. Societies purporting to be repositories of the Eastern wisdom had long instilled a fear of yoga into the minds of their students. Truth seekers were bewildered, having before their eyes no example, until 1920, of a great master, a fully accomplished yogi.

Freedom for India's Soil and Soul

During Yoganandaji's lifetime India won, through nonviolence, her political freedom. But what of the freedom of India's thought to circulate freely in the world without tragic misrepresentation? More than any other man Paramahansaji corrected the Western misconceptions of the ancient Indian teachings.

India's towering spiritual culture, based on man's most ancient and

Rose-blanketed casket with the sacred body of Paramahansa Yogananda, at the last public rites, Self-Realization headquarters, Los Angeles

imperishable scriptures, the *Vedas*, was fostered only by yogis, God-united sages. The most famous of India's sacred books, the *Bhagavad-Gita,* is one long hymn in praise of the divine science of yoga. There Lord Krishna says: "The yogi is greater than body-disciplining ascetics, greater even than the followers of the path of wisdom (*Jnana Yoga*) or of the path of action (*Karma Yoga*); be thou, O disciple Arjuna, a yogi!" (*VI*:46)

Paramahansaji has written in his *Autobiography of a Yogi* (chapter 24): "Yoga has been superficially misunderstood by certain Western writers, but its critics have never been its practitioners.... A yogi engages himself in a definite, step-by-step procedure by which the body and mind are disciplined and the soul gradually liberated. Taking nothing for granted on emotional grounds or by faith, a yogi practices a thoroughly tested series of exercises that were first mapped out by the ancient *rishis*. In every age of India, yoga has produced men who became truly free, true Yogi-Christs.

"Like any other science, yoga is applicable by people of every clime and time. The theory advanced by certain ignorant writers that yoga is 'dangerous' or 'unsuitable' for Westerners is wholly false, and has lamentably deterred many sincere students from seeking its manifold blessings.

"Yoga is a method for restraining the natural turbulence of thoughts, which otherwise impartially prevents all men, of all lands, from glimpsing their true nature of Spirit. Like the healing light of the sun, yoga is beneficial equally to men of the East and to men of the West. The thoughts of most persons are restless and capricious; a manifest need exists for yoga: the science of mind-control!"

The Two Stages of Samadhi or God-Union

Yogananda has given (*Autobiography of a Yogi, chapter 26*) the following explanation of the two authentic stages of *samadhi* (divine communion): "In the initial states of God-communion (*sabikalpa samadhi*) the devotee's consciousness merges in the Cosmic Spirit; his life force is withdrawn from the body, which appears 'dead,' or motionless and rigid. The yogi is fully aware of his bodily condition of suspended animation.

As he progresses to higher spiritual states (*nirbikalpa samadhi*), however, he communes with God without bodily fixation; and in his ordinary waking consciousness, even in the midst of exacting worldly duties."

Only completely liberated masters, those with an outward mission to perform on earth, can remain for years, as did Yoganandaji, in the perfect *nirbikalpa* state of *samadhi*.

The Sanskrit word *bikalpa* means "difference, nonidentity." *Sabikalpa* is the state of *samadhi* "with difference," *nirbikalpa* is the state "without difference." That is, in *sabikalpa samadhi* the devotee still retains a slight feeling of separateness from God; in *nirbikalpa samadhi* he realizes fully his identity as Spirit.

Master seldom entered the *sabikalpa* state. When he did so, it was merely to set an example for the benefit of disciples around him who had not yet attained even that first state of *samadhi* — ecstatic trance or bodily immobilization at the sight of God.

Master's Awe-Inspiring Samadhi in 1948

In June 1948 Paramahansaji passed through a series of the most awe-inspiring states of *samadhi* that his close disciples ever witnessed.* The Hindu scriptures teach that the Impersonal Brahman, the Supreme Spirit, assumes any desired form at the plea of a true devotee. In June 1948 Yoganandaji conversed like a child with the Lord in the aspect of the Divine Mother of the Universe. As She appeared before his inward vision, he poured out his heart to Her, pathetically mentioning many of his little griefs that ordinarily he never referred to in the presence of his disciples. The Mother comforted him tenderly. He asked Her many questions; She used his voice to reply aloud.

The trembling devotees in the room feared the imminence of his

---

*Part of the June 1948 *samadhi* took place while Master was resting on a large brown cloth reclining-type chair. It was on this same chair that Paramahansaji meditated in his sitting room for three hours on March 7, 1952, just before leaving for the Biltmore.

This chair and many other objects with hallowed associations are in Guruji's rooms (now a shrine) at the international headquarters in Los Angeles.

mahasamadhi ("great samadhi" or a yogi's final ecstatic exit from the body). Later he confided that he had hoped at the time that the Beloved Mother would take him. "It was all so perfect!" he said wistfully.

But the Lord apparently had planned a greater stage for the symbolic scenes of His devotee's departure. The public nature of Yoganandaji's death and also its supernatural aftermath appear to be parts of a divine design by which the attention of the world will be drawn more forcefully to the science of yoga.

Very gradually after June 1948 Master clothed his inner state of irrevocable God-union with the outward nature that was dear and familiar to his disciples. He told them at that time: "I shall always be in this state of *nirbikalpa samadhi,* but no one will be able to tell."

Why Perfect Masters Disappear from this Earth

We know from the New Testament that after the crucifixion Christ materialized his physical form, convincing even "doubting Thomas" of its corporeity. We read in *Autobiography of a Yogi* (chapter 36) that "at the morning hour of ten, one day after the body of Lahiri Mahasaya had been consigned to the flames, the resurrected master, in a real but transfigured body, appeared before three disciples, each in a different city." In the same book (chapter 43) we read of Sri Yukteswarji's bodily manifestation after death to comfort his grieving "son" Yoganandaji and to tell him of life on the high astral planet of *Hiranyaloka.* (Sri Yukteswarji now dwells on *Hiranyaloka* as a savior.)

No disciple of Master's who knew him well doubts for an instant that Yoganandaji, too, will reappear on this earth in flesh and blood before those whom God chooses.

It is extremely rare, the Hindu scriptures tell us, for fully emancipated saints to remain for long periods in physical encasement. The ancient Mahavatar Babaji (he who sent Yoganandaji to the New World to disseminate knowledge of the hitherto jealously guarded yogic science) has not yet left his body; nor will he do so, he assures us through his disciples, until the end of the present world cycle. That permanent physical manifestation is a command given to him by God. Nevertheless,

Paramahansa Yogananda, about one hour before his passing, Biltmore Hotel, Los Angeles, March 7, 1952

such an avatar of deathlessness always remains secluded in the world's highest mountains — the Himalayas.

Man's Treatment of Prophets Does Not Make a Proud Record

Once accustomed to the presence on earth of a deathless master, the majority of men would soon fail to pay him the respect that the Lord wishes His perfect devotees to receive. Therefore He removes His saints, by death or by impenetrable seclusion, from the public gaze.

SRI DAYA MATA

The Reverend Mother Daya Mata has been president and spiritual head of Self-Realization Fellowship/Yogoda Satsanga Society of India since 1955 (succeeding Rajarsi Janakananda, the second president).

GOODWIN J. KNIGHT

Lieutenant Governor

STATE OF CALIFORNIA

Los Angeles, California
April 8, 1952

Miss Faye Wright
Self-Realization Fellowship
3880 San Rafael
Los Angeles, California

Dear Miss Wright:

Mrs. Knight and I were indeed shocked and grieved to learn of the sudden demise of our good friend, Paramhansa Yogananda.

Because of the fact that we were at Sacramento for the arduous Legislative Session, it was not possible for us to return to Los Angeles for the last rites for the beloved Master.

We would be glad if you would convey to all of those associated with Master Yogananda in his great work our sincere condolences in the irreparable loss of your leader and founder. His warm personality and kindly understanding will be sorely missed by all of those who were privileged to know him.

Sincerely and faithfully yours,

Goodwin Knight

GOODWIN KNIGHT
Lieutenant Governor

Tributes from Friends and SRF Centers

DR. FRANCIS ROLT-WHEELER, foremost metaphysical scholar of Europe and editor of *L'Astrosophie,* Nice, France, wrote: "The death of Paramahansa Yogananda deprives this world of one of the finest figures of wisdom and humanity that this generation has seen. No one can fail to rejoice that such a life has enriched the spiritual thought of both India and the United States. I feel that Yogananda succeeded in keeping the finer strains of the old tradition, fusing them with the greater vitality of the American present. I shall take pleasure in publishing a tribute to Yogananda in the next issue of *L'Astrosophie,* with a column of his mystic sayings."

DR. BHAGAT SINGH THIND, revered Los Angeles teacher, telegraphed from Chicago: "In the passing away of Yogananda humanity has lost its lover, India a noble son and patriot, and America its true friend and admirer. May God grant courage and loyalty to all his friends and disciples to carry on the great work that he so earnestly fostered with every ounce of energy in his being."

DR. DAGOBERT D. RUNES, president of Philosophical Library, New York, wrote: "It is with great sorrow that I read of the passing of Paramahansa Yogananda. He was a great soul and has left a lasting memory and impression on the cultural life of America."

PROFESSOR TARACHAND ROY, University of Bonn, Germany: "To my unspeakable grief I have just heard of Paramahansaji's demise.... Shelley once wrote: 'The One remains, the many change and pass.' I am convinced that the deathless flame that was Paramahansaji burns undimmed still. He is there now where the Immortals are, and rains down his blessings on all who are holding to his ideals."

DR. WENDELL THOMAS, author of *Hinduism Invades America*, formerly professor at the Punjab University and at the College of the City of New York, wrote: "I came to Swami Yogananda, many years ago, not as a seeker or devotee, but as a writer with a sympathetic yet analytic and critical approach. Happily, I found in Yoganandaji a rare combination. While steadfast in the ancient principles of his profound faith, he had the gift of generous adaptability, so that he became Christian and American in culture without ceasing to be Hindu and Indian. With his quick wit and great spirit he was well fitted to promote reconciliation and truth among the religious seekers of the world. He brought peace and joy to multitudes."

JUDGE STANLEY MOSK, Superior Court, Los Angeles, wrote to SRF: "I was profoundly shocked to witness personally the [heart] attack, and to learn of the subsequent death of a great spiritual leader, Paramahansa Yogananda. From all that I have ever been informed, he was indeed an outstanding individual, devoted to peace and understanding among the peoples of the Earth. It may truly be said that he left the world a little better for his having been on it, if ever so briefly in the totality of events. May I express my condolences to his many faithful followers and friends."

DR. TARAKNATH DAS, Columbia University, New York, telegraphed: "My profound sorrow at passing away of Paramahansa Yogananda. Sympathy to members of Fellowship. Peace."

LOUISE ROYSTON, a beloved disciple of Paramahansaji's since 1927, wrote the following letter to the *Los Angeles Times*, in which it was printed on March 30th: "Thousands of the people of Los Angeles loved Paramahansa Yogananda and mourn his passing. I am just one.

He not only taught us religious principles to follow and practice, but he was a tireless welfare worker. Night and day he toiled to help the sick and the sorrowful. Thousands of people all over America and the whole world have been helped and comforted through his unselfish assistance. He loved America."

SRF CENTER IN SAN FRANCISCO, California. Mrs. Kamala Silva, leader, wrote: "Our Center held memorial services on March 17th. John Laurence gave a short talk saying: 'We must not relax but rather extend our efforts with new resolves, with revitalized enthusiasm. We have had the blessed privilege of a living Master in our midst. His great powers, infinitely extended now in the realm of cosmic bliss and light, are even more available to us than before, for he is yet mindful of his own.'"

SRF STUDENTS IN ROULERS, BELGIUM, wrote: "Paramahansaji's life work has been wonderful and gigantic. What he has given to us — the best of his life and the greatest love of his soul — is enormous. We shall never forget it. He is no more on this earth to lead us through pitfalls of difficulties, but his SRF Lessons stay, to support us daily."

SRF CENTER IN MEXICO CITY. Mr. J.M. Cuaron, leader, wrote "On Tuesday the whole meeting was dedicated to Master. I read several passages from *Whispers from Eternity*. We played Master's songs in the records we have. Then we had a long meditation on him. Afterward everyone was much comforted; most of the students felt the presence of Master in our meeting. I felt not only his presence, but the touch of his hand on my head."

SRF CENTER IN MERIDA, YUCATAN, MEXICO. Mr. Pedro Gonzales Milan, leader, wrote: "I have cried like a child. I feel the death of our Guru more than my father's. Last evening all our members gathered to pay our respects to Master, before a picture of him (when he was young) that I had bought in oil colors. We decorated it with flowers and lighted before it a sacred fire with incense. After chanting our Guru's favorite hymns, I told a short story of Master's life from his childhood to his last days, remembering with love the last SRF Convocation at which I was present.

"On March 18th while I was meditating I felt a strong impression of Master's presence and heard an inner voice say: 'Don't cry. I shall be able to help you now more than before.'"

PROFESSOR VLADIMIR NOVICKY, Prague, Czechoslovakia, wrote: "It is difficult to express in cold human words the depth of our grief as well as our immense gratitude to Paramahansaji, who lit for us a real and tangible light on the path and who showered on us such rich spiritual and material gifts. Every uncertainty, every trouble, and every anxious question sent to him never failed to find a quick response.

"There is no wonder that Paramahansaji departed so soon: he has actually burned himself out in the fire of his selfless service to humanity. He did titanic work. He helped many earnest seekers to find the hidden Light within, to realize their Divine Self, and even to become masters of themselves. We are convinced that SRF will continue its blessed work for suffering mankind ever more intensively and successfully. May our dear Master, in the company of his grand gurus, ever watch over the work and fate of SRF."

SADHAN KUTIR YOGASHRAM, JHARIA, BIHAR, INDIA. The leaders of this Lahiri Mahasaya Ashram wrote: "We herewith send a message from our members, on the departure of the great Rishi Sri Sri Yogananda Paramahansa to the proper place of the yogis: At the holy disappearance of that ever free soul, we are deprived of his direct advice. Today we are faced with the immense responsibility of realizing the purport of his nectarlike speeches. Let us pray to his immortal soul to show us the right path in life."

SERAMPORE COLLEGE, SERAMPORE, WEST BENGAL, INDIA. The principal, Dr. C. E. Abraham, wrote on March 18th. "A condolence meeting was held in the College and speeches were made in Bengali and English, paying tribute to the varied services of Paramahansaji to this College and to the world at large. I know His Holiness had a great love for Serampore College, and the Yogananda Scholarship will stand as a fitting memorial to this fact."

A copy of a resolution of condolence was enclosed. It read as follows: "This meeting of the students and staff of Serampore College, mourning sincerely the death of His Holiness Paramahansa Yogananda, desires to convey its heartfelt condolences to the members of Self-Realization Fellowship in the U.S.A. and to Yogoda Satsanga Society in India, of both of which Paramahansaji was the spiritual head. The Paramahansa was a student at the College, and the College is proud to have on the roll of its alumni such a distinguished person.

"The Paramahansa continued to take an interest in his old College, and recently he has been contributing generously to the funds of the College for the endowment of a scholarship for poor and deserving students. This act shows that the Paramahansa's heart was with the poor, and that, as he worked for the spiritual enlightenment of people according to his best lights, he also worked for the mitigation of various evils in society.

"The College has lost a distinguished old student and friend, and India one of its unofficial ambassadors abroad."

SAB PAYECHIR ASAR, INDIA. The secretary of Sab Payechir Asar, c/o Jugantar, Ltd., Calcutta, wrote: "The sudden passing away of Swamiji came as a rude shock to us, as to many others in India who can boast of the proud privilege of having known him and his great qualities of head and heart. Under the shadow of that national — nay, international — calamity, the members of Sab Payechir Asar assembled at a meeting on March 17th to offer homage to the departed great."

B. C. GUHA, Damodar Valley Corporation, Calcutta, India, wrote: "I had an unforgettable visit with Paramahansaji in America for two or three days in January, 1945. His kindness, affection, and all embracing humanitarianism won my heart. I have no doubt that his spirit will still pervade your organization and help the unity of nations at higher and still higher levels."

SRI BHUPENDRA NATH SARKAR, educationist, writer, and friend of Self-Realization Fellowship, wrote in the Calcutta *Hindustan Standard*: "The Fellowship he established aimed at two things: contact

(*Continued on page 125*)

Forest Lawn Memorial-Park

Glendale 5, California

TELEPHONES:
LOS ANGELES, CLEVELAND 6-3131
GLENDALE CITRUS 1-4151
CABLE ADDRESS HUBERT-LOS ANGELES

May 16, 1952

Self-Realization Fellowship
3880 San Rafael Avenue
Los Angeles 65
California

Gentlemen:

   The absence of any visual signs of decay in the dead body of Paramhansa Yogananda offers the most extraordinary case in our experience. Had the muscle protein and blood stream of the deceased not been comparatively free of bacteria, deterioration of the body could have set in as early as six hours after life had departed. No physical disintegration was visible in Paramhansa Yogananda's body even twenty days after death.

   The body was under daily observation at the Mortuary of the Forest Lawn Memorial-Park Association from March 11, 1952, the day of the last public rites, until March 27, 1952, when the bronze casket was sealed by fire. During this period no indication of mold was visible on Paramhansa Yogananda's skin, and no visible desiccation (drying up) took place in the bodily tissues. This state of perfect preservation of a body is, so far as we know from mortuary annals, an unparalleled one.

   Officials of Forest Lawn viewed the body of Paramhansa Yogananda an hour after his death on March 7, 1952. The body was then taken to his home on Mount Washington in Los Angeles, where many friends gathered to gaze at his form.

   For protection of the public health, embalming is desirable if a dead body is to be exposed for several days to public view. Embalming of the body of Paramhansa Yogananda took place twenty-four hours after his demise. In normal room-temperature, the enzyme action of the intestines of deceased persons causes distention of the tissues in the abdominal region about six hours after death. Such distention did not occur at any time in the case of Paramhansa Yogananda. When our Mortuary received his body for embalming, it presented no signs of physical deterioration and no putrefactive odor -- two very unusual absences when a death has occurred twenty-four hours earlier.

Paramhansa Yogananda's body was embalmed on the night of March 8th, with that quantity of fluid which is customarily used in any body of similar size. No unusual treatment was given.

In cases of persons that are embalmed and exhibited to friends for a period of two or three weeks, it is necessary, to insure presentability, for the embalmer to apply, on the face and hands of the deceased, a creamy pore-sealing emulsion that temporarily prevents the outward appearance of mold. In Paramhansa Yogananda's case, however, no emulsions were used. They were superfluous, inasmuch as his tissues underwent no visible transformations.

After embalming on the night of March 8th, the body of Paramhansa Yogananda was returned to the Self-Realization Fellowship headquarters on Mount Washington. At the final public rites there on the afternoon of March 11th, the glass sealer lid of the bronze coffin was fastened securely and was not again removed. His body was never touched again by human hands.

The body in the casket was taken about 10 p.m. on March 11th to our Mortuary for daily observation. The reason for this procedure was the hope of Self-Realization Fellowship officers that two disciples of Paramhansa Yogananda's from India might arrive in Los Angeles some time in March, when they could be brought to the Mortuary to view the body.

In any sealed casket, into which air cannot enter and from which air cannot escape, the internal moisture of the dead body, whether embalmed or unembalmed, soon forms a white mold on the skin unless the protective cream, not used in this case, is used. The natural characteristic of the muscle protein is to break down into amino acids and then into ptomaine acids. When ptomaine acids become active, deterioration of tissues is rapid. Paramhansa Yogananda's body was apparently devoid of any impurities by which muscle proteins could be resolved into ptomaine acids. His tissues remained intact.

At the time of receiving Paramhansa Yogananda's body, the Mortuary personnel at Forest Lawn expected to observe, through the glass lid of the casket, the usual progressive signs of bodily decay. Our astonishment increased as day followed day without bringing any visible change in the body under observation. Paramhansa Yogananda's body was apparently in a phenomenal state of immutability.

On the late morning of March 26th, we observed a very slight, a barely noticeable, change -- the appearance on the tip of the nose of a brown spot, about one-fourth inch in diameter. This small faint spot indicated that the process of desiccation (drying up) might finally be starting. No visible mold appeared, however.

The hands at all times remained normal in size, revealing no signs of shriveling or pinching at the fingertips -- the place where desiccation is ordinarily seen very early. The lips, which wore a slight smile, continuously retained their firmness. No odor of decay emanated from Paramhansa Yogananda's body at any time. Although the casket was closed by the heavy glass lid, it was not hermetically sealed. Any odor from the deceased, had it been present, would have been immediately detected by persons standing near the coffin. The volatile nature of odors renders it impossible to conceal their presence, except in rare circumstances that did not here obtain.

As word had been received that the two disciples from India would not be coming to America until 1953, the officers of Self-Realization Fellowship agreed, on March 27, 1952, that entombment of Paramhansa's casket should now take place. The inner glass lid was therefore sealed by fire to the lower part of the casket; the massive bronze cover was then placed on top and secured with mastic sealer and with bolts. The process of sealing by fire was accomplished on March 27th and 28th. The casket was removed on March 28, 1952, to a crypt in the Great Mausoleum in Forest Lawn Memorial-Park, to remain there until such time as permanent enshrinement of the body can be arranged for by the Self-Realization Fellowship.

The physical appearance of Paramhansa Yogananda on March 27th, just before the bronze cover of the casket was put into position, was the same as it had been on March 7th. He looked on March 27th as fresh and as unravaged by decay as he had looked on the night of his death. On March 27th there was no reason to say that his body had suffered any visible physical disintegration at all. For these reasons we state again that the case of Paramhansa Yogananda is unique in our experience.

On May 11, 1952, during a telephone conversation between an officer of Forest Lawn and an officer of Self-Realization Fellowship, the whole amazing story was brought out for the first time. Previously the Fellowship officer had not known the details, as he had not been in touch with the Mortuary Director but only with the Administrative Department of Forest Lawn. In the interests of truth, we are glad to present this written account for publication in Self-Realization Magazine.

Yours sincerely,

FOREST LAWN MEMORIAL-PARK ASSOCIATION, INC.

By *Harry T. Rowe*
Harry T. Rowe, Mortuary Director

Self-Realization Fellowship
May 16, 1952
Page Four

STATE OF CALIFORNIA,   )
)   ss.
COUNTY OF LOS ANGELES.)

     On the 16th day of May, 1952 before me, Maxine
Chapman, a Notary Public in and for said County and State
personally appeared Harry T. Rowe, known to me to be the
Mortuary Director of Forest Lawn Memorial-Park Association,
Inc. and acknowledged to me that as such Mortuary Director
he signed the foregoing letter dated May 16, 1952 addressed
to the Self-Realization Fellowship at 3880 San Rafael Avenue,
Los Angeles 65, California.

     IN WITNESS WHEREOF I have hereunto set my hand and
affixed my official seal this day and year first above written.

                          Maxine Chapman
                  Notary Public in and for said
                       County and State
              My Commission Expires February 4, 1956

(Continued from page 120)

with God through knowledge of the self as a divine spark of God, and fellowship with all mankind. Verily, Yogananda was attempting a sadly needed readjustment between the spiritual and the material plane, by harmonizing science and religion through realization of their underlying unity. Paramahansa Yogananda worked miracles. I still remember his magnetic personality beaming through his eyes and talks. I dubbed him a messenger of the East to the West. Indeed, he showed the way to happiness to all his fellow beings. India is proud of her son, so noble, loving, divinely human and cosmopolitan."

YSS CENTER, MADRAS, INDIA. "Yoganandaji was verily a rock — nay, a mountain of faith from which poured a perennial flow of inspirational words to touch the hearts of his many disciples. Numerous incidents in his life go to show the power of faith and prayer to accomplish good and to heal physical and mental diseases. None of us who have read his *Autobiography* can think of him as dead. He must have chosen a different plane of living to help us all more effectively. May he be showering on us his divine blessings!"

RANCHI SCHOOL (YSS *Brahmacharya Vidyalaya*), Ranchi, Bihar, high school with yoga training, founded by Yoganandaji in 1917. "We the Indian disciples of Paramahansaji share your profound sorrow at the demise of our great Gurudev who was a living God to us. Not only was he a great religious teacher, preaching the highest ideals of India's ancient culture, but also a wonderful patriot in whom India found a true son. We feel his omnipresent soul with us still, guiding us in all our right activities. We have lost the presence of his earthly body but find his spirit ever glowing within our hearts. Our Gurudev Paramahansa Yoganandaji was a living example of universal love and brotherhood, a personified spirit of unity between India and America, a true exemplar of the best in East and West."

BOOKS BY PARAMAHANSA YOGANANDA

Available at or through your local bookstore, or directly from the publisher: Self-Realization Fellowship, 3880 San Rafael Avenue, Los Angeles, California 90065

Please request current catalog before ordering

Autobiography of a Yogi
Man's Eternal Quest
The Science of Religion
Whispers from Eternity
Songs of the Soul
Sayings of Paramahansa Yogananda
Scientific Healing Affirmations
How You Can Talk With God
Metaphysical Meditations
The Law of Success
Cosmic Chants

Other Publications

The Holy Science
By Swami Sri Yukteswar

"Only Love"
By Sri Daya Mata

God Alone: The Life and Letters of a Saint
—Sri Gyanamata

"Mejda": The Family and the Early Life of
Paramahansa Yogananda
By Sananda Lal Ghosh

"Undreamed-of Possibilities"
Introductory booklet available on request